Learning to *Fly*

Timothy Coker

Learning to Fly

Copyright 2019 Timothy Coker

All Rights Reserved

All scripture references, unless otherwise noted, are from the New American Standard Bible (NASB).

ISBN: 978-1-940645-69-8

Greenville, South Carolina

PUBLISHED IN THE UNITED STATES OF AMERICA

This book is for those who have not yet learned how to fly according to God's plan. It is for those who dread each day, struggle with less than ideal circumstances, or are having difficulty dealing with those around them.
God has a plan for you, and it is good!

Contents

Acknowledgments	vii
Introduction	ix
PART ONE:	
DEALING WITH THE INTERNAL THINGS THAT PREVENT YOU FROM FLYING	
1 — The God Who Wants More for You	15
2 — Waiting for Take Off	23
3 — Facing Our Fears	33
4 — Oops! I Have Failed (Part I)	47
5 — Oops! I Have Failed (Part II)	55
PART TWO:	
DEALING WITH EXTERNAL THINGS THAT PREVENT YOU FROM FLYING	
6 — Learning to Forgive	63
7 — A Marriage That Gets It	73
8 — Then Comes Baby in a Baby Carriage	83
9 — When I Don't Get What I Want	91
10 — On Your Mark! Get Set! Grow!	99
11 — What Do You Do with Ghosts?	109
Conclusion	115
Notes	117

Acknowledgments

I would not be able to do much of anything, let alone write, if it were not for my wife, Donna. Thank you for truly being with me.

I am also grateful for Christopher and Ashton. Thank you for loving me — even when my walk has not matched my talk.

I am also thankful to my personal accountability team, and my inner circle of friends. All of you have read/edited/encouraged parts of this manuscript.

I have been blessed by the three congregations the Lord has allowed me to pastor. I am incredibly thankful to Central Baptist Church of Darlington, both staff and congregation. For twenty-three years, you have shown me how to fly!

I owe humble thanks to Wayne and Rodney for listening to my whines, and owe a special debt to John Isgett ... you know why.

Finally, I am blessed to say a special thank you to Regina Smeltzer, writer par excellence, editor, confidante and friend. God used you to bless my life!

Introduction

There is a big difference between traveling by air and flying. I have been on many trips, have boarded many planes, and I know the difference. Those who *travel* have a different approach than those who *fly*. The two groups of people have different goals. They have different values, different concerns.

Those who travel by air rush from gate to gate as if they are part of a pit crew changing a tire at the Daytona 500. They browse at no shops, eat no snacks, and smile at no passersby. They board their planes with a certain amount of dread and stoically take their seats. They have been through this before and know what to expect. Lousy peanuts. Lousy movie. Loud child sitting beside them. They just want the trip to be over.

Those who *fly*, on the other hand, are different. They laugh. They eat. They browse. They eat. They watch others. They enjoy the scenery. They eat! *Flyers* take delight in the trip. They take delight in their seats. They enjoy the peanuts and the movies. And, yes, they even enjoy the child sitting next them. Flyers drive everyone else crazy! It's as if they are privy to a secret that no one else knows. Someone has taught them how to enjoy travel, and it's not fair!

Do you fly or merely travel?

What is true in air transportation is also true in life. There are flyers, and there are travelers. One enjoys the life-trip, while the other stoically gets through it. One delights in the experience, while the other hates it. One soars, while the other merely exists.

Imagine a life where you rise above your negative circumstances, soar above the issues — both personal and situational — that rob you of the joy that should be yours. Imagine a life where you not only fly, but you are in the cockpit and God is your co-pilot. No one is born knowing how to fly. But flying can be learned.

This book is for those who have not yet learned how to fly. If you dread each day, or struggle with less than ideal circumstances, or if you are having difficulty dealing with those around you, then this book is written for you. It is not a book on theology, or an exposition of scripture. It is a book about life, written by one who is still learning to enjoy the trip. My prayer is that God will teach you the secret of navigating life. My hope is that you will *Learn to Fly!*

Timothy Coker
September 2019

Learning to *Fly*

PART ONE

Dealing with the Internal Things that Prevent You from Flying

Isaiah 40:28-31

*Do you not know? Have you not heard?
The Everlasting God, the Lord, the Creator of the ends of the earth
Does not become weary or tired.
His understanding is inscrutable.
He gives strength to the weary,
And to him who lacks might He increases power.
Though youths grow weary and tired,
And vigorous young men stumble badly,
Yet those who wait for the Lord
Will gain new strength;
They will mount up with wings like eagles,
They will run and not get tired,
They will walk and not become weary.*

1

THE GOD WHO WANTS MORE FOR YOU

I know this book is about learning to fly, but let me relate flying to another passion of mine. I don't know about you, but I am a big fan of the *Matrix Trilogy*. I saw *The Matrix* in a theater for the first time several years ago. Though I did not like everything about the movie, I was fascinated by the theme.

Neo, the hero of *The Matrix*, discovers that most human beings have been reduced to "energy-producing nothings" who are unaware that the world they believe to be real is actually a computer-generated figment of someone's imagination. Machines govern the Matrix — they control it. Neo, along with a few other humans, escapes the Matrix and discovers the real world. Neo is no longer bound by the restrictions and limits created by those around him. He discovers true freedom, purpose and meaning. At one point in the trilogy, someone asks, "Have you seen Neo?" The reply: "He's doing his Superman thing again." Neo is soaring above the world! He has learned how to fly.

Sound inviting? Wouldn't it be great to live life by a different set of rules? Wouldn't it be nice to soar above your world … or circumstances … or problems … or doubts? Can you imagine being able to fly? Can you see yourself soaring, living a life different from those trapped in a culture of "energy-producing nothings"?

God can fathom it. He wants you to fly. He wants it *for* you. Did you catch that little three-letter word? *For*. Not from, but *for* you.

From you means God demands.

For you means God gives.

From means we fall short.

For means God provides.

From means we live frustrated, unable to fly.

For means we live on a new level of joy. God speaks of this new level in His Word:

> **But those** *who wait on the LORD shall renew their strength;*
> *They shall mount up with wings like eagles,*
> *They shall run and not be weary,*
> *They shall walk and not faint (Isaiah 40:31).*

"But those" implies that there are others — others who don't wait on the LORD, others who get faint and weary, others who fall (Isaiah 40:30). There are others living among us who will, regardless of age, intellect or riches, never escape Matrix living.

Most of us don't want to fall. We are sick of being weary. So what do we need to know about this God who wants us to fly? God, who wants more for each of us, is a God of relationships, a God of risks and a God of rewards.

The God Who Wants More for You Is a God of Relationships

You cannot fly on your own. In order to fly, you must become involved in a special relationship with God. This relationship isn't about church membership, family tradition, denominational involvement or social standing. It is about God and you. "Those who wait on the Lord" — and only those who wait on the Lord — "will mount up with wings like eagles" (Isaiah 40:31).

The Hebrew word for "wait" in Isaiah 40:30 is *qavah*, which means "to bind or twist together." *Qavah* is also used in Psalm 56:6, where it means "to lie in wait." You can find this word, *qavah*, again in Jeremiah 3:17, where its meaning is "to gather or collect." Based on these definitions, some scholars think that there are two separate Hebrew words that look alike with entirely different meanings.[1] I disagree. Does *qavah* mean "to bind," or "lie in wait"? Or does it mean "to twist" or "gather"? Yes! It means all of these.

Have you ever had a friend with whom you were more apt to get into trouble when you were together than when you were alone? Were there things you would try only if your buddy was there?

I had a friend like that. We were twisted together so tightly that we would try anything if we were by each other's side. I never would have jumped out at the neighbors' kids on Halloween, but Gary and I did. I never would have knocked on the neighbors' doors and ran, but Gary and I did. I would shrink back in fear at the thought of fighting the bullies down the street — but when Gary came over, we'd give it a try! I would wait until we were together to attempt most of my acts of daring. That's what *qavah* means.

God wants you to be so twisted — so close to Him — that you'll wait for Him before you try any daring acts. He wants to be so close to you that you won't try anything until He and you are together. Think of this as tandem sky diving. Alone, the unskilled will fall to their deaths. But connected to God, they fly!

God wants that for you. He wants a relationship — the relationship of all relationships. He wants you to not simply travel through life, but to fly! He's made it possible through Jesus Christ. So, before we do any more "flight training," you need to have this one-of-a-kind relationship. If you have never made a decision to follow Jesus, I hope you will admit that you are a sinner, not necessarily because of gross, terrible actions, but by an attitude of "I don't need you, God." Pause and quietly receive His love and forgiveness.

If you are already a believer, take time now to submit yourself again to God's control.

Please take a few moments in prayer with the greatest flight instructor of all.

THE GOD WHO WANTS MORE FOR YOU IS A GOD OF RISKS

Once we enter a relationship with God, He wants us to experience life on a new level. No more being stuck in the Matrix. No more trying to fly, only to fall on our faces. No more playing it safe. No more boring. No more predictability. He wants us to soar like eagles, to rise above our fear and experience the thrill of victory!

But wait. Eagles fly higher than other birds. And the higher you fly, the farther you fall!

The Bible records many stories about people who were called to take risks. Some of them risked their reputations. Some of them risked their careers. Others risked their lives. Noah risked his reputation, building a ship (for 120 years!) in a world that had never experienced rain. Elijah risked his career, boldly speaking the truth before a hostile king. David risked his life, when, armed only with a slingshot, he went into battle with a giant.

How about it? Are you ready to take risks for God? Are you ready to fly higher and see more? I know what you are thinking: *The*

Christians I know are the most boring people in the world. They don't look like risk-takers to me. Or you may be thinking: *What about all those Christians who never take a risk?* I ask you, what about all those Christians who do?

I remember the first time I took a BIG risk. I was a young boy (six or seven years of age), living in Corpus Christi, Texas. Those of us in the neighborhood passed the time by climbing trees. There was one stand of trees — chinaberry trees — which were especially tall. Those chinaberry trees were also spindly. Their limbs waved and extended like skeletons' arms — scary, but perfect for climbing.

My friends and I scaled those creatures, climbed out on the protruding limbs and then dropped to the earth below. Nothing was impossible. No limb was too high. No drop too far.

And then Lee spotted it: way up there … perhaps beyond the snow line … far beyond the realm of possibility — *the Limb of Limbs*. We called it "Apollo," because there was a greater chance of man walking on the moon than of us making that drop.

I thought about scaling to Apollo for days. I studied it. I "philosophized" on it. I weighed the pros and cons, and realized that the only way to experience the thrill of victory was to risk the agony of defeat.

I arose early that morning, walked down the street to the corner, took one last look up at Apollo, and began my ascent. Before I reached the pinnacle, my friends had gathered. Failed climbers from yesteryear joined them. Walter Cronkite was below (well, not really).

I reached the mighty limb, Apollo.

I swung out and wrapped my two skinny arms around it.

I hung for what seemed like years, the fear soaking my brain faster than sweat soaked my back.

Then I let go — and crashed to the earth with a thud. I looked around to see if I was in heaven. I was not; I was alive! And I was famous! I had conquered Apollo!

I never forgot that morning because I learned a great lesson that day: There is no flight without some fright. There is no cheering without a challenge.

What "Apollo" do you have in your life that needs conquering? Take a risk. Share the "Apollo" with God. Battle it in tandem flight. Only then can you truly fly.

The God Who Wants More for You Is a God of Rewards

When we conquer our "Apollos," our lives will never be the same. "Those who wait on the Lord shall **renew their strength**. They shall run and not be weary. They shall walk and not faint" (Isaiah 40:31). The Hebrew word for "renew" could also mean "to exchange" — exchange our weakness for His strength, our fatigue for His energy and our inability for His ability. I love the way the Apostle Paul spoke of this "exchanging" in 1 Corinthians 1:26-27:

> *Take a good look, friends, at who you were when you got called into this life. I don't see many of the "brightest and the best" among you, not many influential, not many from high-society families. Isn't it obvious that God deliberately chose men and women that the culture overlooks and exploits and abuses, chose these "nobodies" to expose the hollow pretensions of the "somebodies"? (Eugene Peterson's The Message).*

Is Paul describing you? Are you the person that culture overlooks? The one society exploits or abuses? Do you feel like a "nobody"?

If so, I have great news! You are a candidate for renewal. You can be "exchanged." God is the giver of rewards!

Perhaps you know the story of William Wilberforce. History remembers him as the Christian statesman who led the fight against slavery in the British Empire, but his peers remember a tiny, soft-spoken man who allowed God to exchange his strength. The writer James Boswell once said of William Wilberforce: "I saw what seemed to me a shrimp become a whale."[2] What a wonderful picture of what can happen to a man or a woman when we wait on God.

Tired of being a shrimp? Want to do some exchanging? Would you like to become a whale? There is only one way, and that is God's way. He wants to become your flight instructor.

Say "yes" to Him, and enter the greatest relationship you'll ever know.

Say "yes" to Him, and live a life of risks.

Say "yes" to Him, and say goodbye to the Matrix and its tired, ho-hum way of life.

Say "yes" to Him! Come on, get your reward. Let's go flying!

But before we can fly, we have to **take off …**

Psalm 62:1-5

My soul waits in silence for God only;
From Him is my salvation. He only is my rock and my salvation,
My stronghold; I shall not be greatly shaken.
How long will you assail a man,
That you may murder him, all of you,
Like a leaning wall, like a tottering fence?
They have counseled only to thrust them down from his high position;
They delight in falsehood;
They bless with their mouth,
But inwardly they curse. Selah.
My soul, wait in silence for God only,
For my hope is from Him.

Waiting for Take Off

No one knows instinctively how to fly. It is not something coded in our DNA, or passed on at the dinner table, parent to child. Mastering the ability to fly takes time and practice. How we make decisions as we master this new skill is an important part of learning to fly.

We had already spent an eternity at the Barbie aisle of Walmart. I was tired. My mind wearied. My little girl, Ashton, and I had gone out to dinner together. My wife and son were out-of-town on a field trip.

"Where would you like to eat?" I asked while we were still at home.

"How about Western Sizzlin?" she replied.

Something was wrong. Ashton would never choose a steak house, especially with all the McDonald's we'd drive by to get there.

"Why Western Sizzlin?" There had to be a catch.

"Well, I thought we could go out to eat — and then we could go to Walmart and buy me a toy! I love you, Daddy!"

That's how I found myself at the Barbie aisle of the toy department.

"Ashton, choose one or the other." Impatience laced my words. She was torn between a piece of Barbie furniture for her dollhouse ($5.00) or a new Barbie ($12.00). I secretly hoped the furniture would win out. "We have to be going, sweetheart, so make a decision."

With time pressuring her, and with her daddy compelling her, Ashton reverted to the method of decision-making taught by sages and magi for centuries. "Eeny meeny miny mo, catch a tiger by his toe …." She pointed her finger back and forth from the furniture to the doll.

I could not believe it! My precious girl was going to make the biggest decision of her day a matter of chance, not thought. I watched her finger stop on the furniture (and not on the doll). She turned and said, "Daddy, let's do this over." She proceeded to start the selection process again. Guess who bought a doll that night?

That was many years ago. Ashton is a young adult now, but the memory stays with me. How much she is like me — perhaps like you, too — leaving decisions to fate. If you are going to learn to fly, you must find a way to consciously make godly choices. You must not make the biggest decisions of your day — and life — by chance.

David was a man who knew about decisions. Good ones. Bad ones. Great choices. Poor choices. The battle with Goliath. The sin with Bathsheba. Wonderful victories. Agonizing consequences. He knew them all. Read David's words in the Psalms. Like David, you must answer three questions in order to continue your flight training: Will you wait, will you listen, and will you live it out?

Will You Wait?

The Hebrew translation of the opening of Psalm 62 is: "Only for God in silence does my soul wait." The first question that you must answer in order to make godly decisions is, "Will you wait?" Can you accept the fact that "wait" means WAIT?

There are several Hebrew words used in the Bible for the word "wait." In Psalm 62:1, the word "wait" implies "rest, pondering, looking ahead." Wait does not mean "do nothing," but it does mean "wait"!

Waiting for Take Off

Waiting is my least favorite subject to preach, teach or discuss. I don't have a handle on this "waiting deal," as one of my friends calls it, nor do I consider myself an expert in this area. I have learned through experiences, mostly by mistakes, that when I ignore God's way of making decisions, I pay a great price! I am still learning. And I still hate to wait.

We all hate to wait, do we not? How about these reminders: traffic … the doctor's office … the football game … the restaurant … the airport … the grocery store? We'll do almost anything to avoid waiting. We'll settle for less, and sometimes settle for wrong, rather than wait.

Have you ever spent an entire week looking forward to Friday night and a visit to your local steak house? Earlier in the week, you declined invitations ("No, I can't … I'm going out to eat on Friday"). You saved your money. You dressed for the occasion. You reviewed the menu in your mind. You fantasized about the taste of the A1 … the salad … the baked potato … the rolls … the sweet tea! (Enough! I'm feeling hungry.)

You are in the car, excited to get there! As you drive up to your favorite restaurant, you notice the crowds on the front porch and the lines inside. The hostess tells you it will be forty-five minutes until you can be seated, and … YOU DECIDE TO GO TO ANOTHER RESTAURANT!

I'm not waiting. I don't care if it is my favorite place to eat! I don't care if I have been looking forward to this night all week. You say goodbye to the A1, the salad, the sweet tea, and settle for a hot dog at Bubba's Barbeque!

You've been waiting a hundred hours. Couldn't you wait one more? No, because we hate to wait! It is not natural. Waiting is not the way of our culture.

We do not like to wait on God, either. No wonder we make some crazy decisions. We make decisions in *our* time based on *our* thinking. In order to make godly decisions, we must build into our lives some slow-down time. We need the patience to wait until God speaks.

We must decide to wait for and rest in God. Wait means WAIT!

Will You Listen to Him First?

The second question that you must ask yourself when approaching a decision is, "Will I seek Him, and listen to Him, first?"

"Only **for God in silence** does my soul wait!" (Psalm 62:1, bold emphasis mine). God is the first one you must seek. The reason for this is found in Psalm 62:2: "Because He is my defense. He is my rock. He is my refuge. He is my shelter. He is my salvation." He … He … He! Let me put those words in street talk: He can get it done. He alone can get it done.

As a pastor, people seek me for counseling. Sometimes their lives are really messed up. Other times they are looking for guidance.

"Tim, what should I do?"

"How can I solve this problem?"

"How can I undo this poor decision?"

I love them. I encourage them. I hope to help them. But I can't solve their problems because I am not their rock, their shelter, their refuge, or their salvation. I cannot get it done; only God can. So I pray with them.

This is why it is important to wait for God. He cannot be one of many voices you listen to; He must be the *first* voice you listen to!

I realize this is opposite from our culture's thinking. Many people, even Christians, believe that God doesn't really speak. Most of our prayers happen with us doing the talking, not God. But if we take a look at the biblical picture of prayer, we notice it is more conversational. God speaks as much as we do.

The skeptic in you asks, "But how do I hear Him if He is silent?"

Let's go back to Psalm 62:1. In this passage, the Hebrew word for "silence" actually means "whisper." It is like two lovers sharing an intimate moment, with one whispering in the other's ear. Brenda Lee did a song in the '50s called *Sweet Nothings:*

My baby whispers in my ear ... ooh, sweet nothings.
He knows the things I like to hear ... ooh, sweet nothings.
Things he wouldn't tell nobody else,
Secrets, baby, I keep them to myself.
Sweet nothings ... ooh, sweet nothings!

If you are married, then you know what I am talking about. You and your spouse have that kind of relationship. You and your spouse speak your own special language. You say things to each other that you would never share with friends or neighbors. It's as if yours is a unique relationship, because it is! I always challenge young ladies who are struggling with the decision to marry to consider the "Sweet Nothings" issue. If your fiancée or boyfriend does not whisper — if, as a couple, you do not speak your own language — then don't get married! He probably will not change. This type of intimacy in a relationship doesn't come naturally. It comes only after an investment of time and effort. It is directly related to a partner's ability (usually the husband's) to listen!

The same is true of our intimacy with the Lord. I believe David had that kind of relationship with God. He was able to hear the "Sweet Somethings" of his Maker.

In other words, silence is not God's response, it is ours. We are to be the *listeners*. He is to be the *speaker*. We must learn to hear and discern His "Sweet Somethings." Just as you must make an effort to listen to your spouse, or closest friends, so you must invest in your heavenly relationship. It takes work, and it is not (if I may repeat myself) natural!

Will You Live It Out?

The final question that must be answered in order to make good decisions is, "Will I live out what I believe God is saying to me?"

"How do I know when I hear *His* voice?" you ask. "How can I act on something if I'm not sure?"

Have you ever wondered that? Have you ever doubted? Have you ever talked yourself out of doing the wise thing, not sure if it was God speaking? I have, and because of this I have made some monumental mistakes through the years — even after praying.

So, I came up with a safeguard or filter that I use when I begin to doubt God's voice. It is called the "Garden Tomb" test. On my first trip to Jerusalem, as I leaned on a rail outside of the Garden Tomb (by the way, there *is* a Presence there, and it is a very emotional place), I reflected on how God had blessed me. *What would my life be like*, I wondered, *if I did not believe in Jesus?* And then I thought, *How has my life been different because I do believe?*

What I use in a reflective way can also be used in a projective way. I ask myself: "What will my decision be if I truly believe this is His voice? Does it require that I trust in Him ... or live out my beliefs ... or place my faith in His provision?" God will never send you in a direction that doesn't call you to trust ... or obey ... or believe.

Let me share a time when He came through for me. I am willing to also share many failures, times when I got it wrong (call me, and I'll be glad to talk to you about them), but now I want to tell of a time when I got it right.

It was October 1984. I was in the Air Force, stationed in Montana, working on nuclear missiles. I had every intention of spending twenty years in the service, but God had other plans. He called me to preach.

I found an Air Force program that would release me from full-time military service and commit me, instead, to the National Guard. If accepted into the program, I could leave Montana early and begin my seminary education in January. The plan seemed perfect. I found a guard unit (McIntyre Air National Guard in Columbia) that would accept my skill sets, filled out the paperwork, and was tentatively approved. One thing remained: a personal interview with the Commander of the McIntyre Air National Guard Unit.

So, in late October I flew to South Carolina for the interview. As I sat outside of the Commander's office, waiting for the Colonel to welcome me, a strange thought entered my mind. *What are you going to tell him when he asks why you want to transfer into his unit? You aren't really going to tell him that God has called you to preach, and that you want to start school early, are you? These "gung ho" military types don't care about your personal plans.* Maybe it was fear. Maybe it was self-doubt. Maybe it was the devil. Suddenly, I didn't know what to do.

I walked into the Colonel's office and sat down. After a few minutes of simple conversation, he looked over his desk and inquired, "Tell me, Sergeant Coker, why do you wish to join our guard unit at McIntyre?" Sweat beaded on my head and my throat tightened. As I sat there for what seemed like months, I remembered the Proverb, "Trust in the Lord with all your heart … and lean not on your own understanding." I thought, *Tim, God has taken care of all this stuff from the beginning. If He doesn't want your transfer approved, He knows what's best.* I took a gulp and said, "Sir, I am tempted to tell you that I want to make a career out of the National Guard, and that this is the best unit in the area. The truth is, Colonel, that God has called me to preach. I am leaving the military to begin school in January. I want to get to the seminary as fast as possible."

The Colonel leaned back, exposing a picture on his wall. It was a bird and a flower. There was a verse of scripture on the canvas: "Trust in the Lord with all your heart and lean not on your own understanding." I gasped. He smiled, and then said, "You have come to the right place. I am a Christian, too." He ended the interview and signed the approval form.

Am I telling you that God is always going to work everything out the way you want it? Am I telling you that there will never be heartache or struggles in your life? Am I telling you that you will never make poor decisions? No.

I am telling you that God is *real,* and that He *cares about you.* I am telling you that He longs to be involved in your decision-making and that if you answer these three questions with reasonable clarity — Will you wait? Will you listen? Will you live it out? — you'll have less confusion discerning His will. No more "eeny meeny miny mo" for you! You'll be making godly decisions by ... waiting ... listening ... soaring!

So, if you are waiting for Him, and listening for His voice in prayer, and have an answer that demands that you live out your beliefs ... Go for it! It's Him! He'll come through!

Exodus 14:10-16

As Pharaoh drew near, the sons of Israel looked, and behold, the Egyptians were marching after them, and they became very frightened; so the sons of Israel cried out to the Lord. Then they said to Moses, "Is it because there were no graves in Egypt that you have taken us away to die in the wilderness? Why have you dealt with us in this way, bringing us out of Egypt? "Is this not the word that we spoke to you in Egypt, saying, 'Leave us alone that we may serve the Egyptians'? For it would have been better for us to serve the Egyptians than to die in the wilderness." But Moses said to the people, "Do not fear! Stand by and see the salvation of the Lord which He will accomplish for you today; for the Egyptians whom you have seen today, you will never see them again forever. The Lord will fight for you while you keep silent." Then the Lord said to Moses, "Why are you crying out to Me? Tell the sons of Israel to go forward. As for you, lift up your staff and stretch out your hand over the sea and divide it, and the sons of Israel shall go through the midst of the sea on dry land."

3

FACING OUR FEARS

While in seminary, I heard the old Indian fable of a mouse in constant distress because of its fear of the cat. A magician took pity on the mouse and turned it into a cat. Immediately, it became afraid of the dog, so the magician turned it into a dog. Then it began to fear the tiger, so the magician turned it into a tiger. Instantly, it began to fear the hunter. The magician said, "I cannot help you, for though you have the body of a tiger, you possess the heart of a mouse."[3]

Is this a picture of you, a child of God with the heart of a mouse? If you are going to fly — experience life the way God means for you to experience it — you must learn to overcome your fears. Fear holds us to the ground, keeps us from experiencing the lift that God provides.

There are two ways to approach fear. One is the worldly way, and the other is the godly way. One way survives fear, while the other faces it. Let's call the worldly way the "lights out" approach.

Have you ever been in the house when the electricity failed? Living in South Carolina for many years, it is not uncommon in the spring to face late evening thunderstorms. The wind comes up, the lightning flashes, and the thunder rumbles so loud that the windows vibrate. Sometimes the electricity fails and the lights go out. In the darkness, the entire world changes. Children awaken and cry out in fear, grown-ups rush to find flashlights, candles, matches or screaming children — anything to restore peace!

I have played both parts, screaming child and panicked parent. As a child, I felt the terror of lying in the dark, expecting each flash of lightning to bring the end of life as I knew it. I have also played the role of panicked parent, bumping into furniture that had not moved, hitting door frames with my face, and wandering through my house as if it was an unfamiliar hotel. Life becomes chaos until we find a light. Then we ride out the storm. Within the next couple of hours, the electricity is restored and we go back to sleep. Life is normal again. Until the next storm hits — and the lights go out again!

In the "lights out" approach to handling fear, we bounce from one episode to another, one trial after the other, panicking in the dark, hoping to find the light. This way of dealing with fear never works, so there must be another option. And there is. It is God's way! It is more than the way of survival; it is the way of victory!

In the story in Exodus 14, after many plagues and many signs of God's strength, Pharaoh finally told Moses and the Hebrew nation to get out of Egypt. Shortly after the Hebrews left, Pharaoh's heart was once again hardened and he decided to pursue them. Pharaoh chased them with "six hundred choice chariots, all the chariots of Egypt, with captains over every one of them" (v. 7). In other words, he brought everything he had. Isn't that the way Satan usually hits us, too, with everything he has?

Pharaoh trapped the Hebrews by the Red Sea. Exodus 14:10 tells us: "And when Pharaoh drew near, the children of Israel lifted their eyes, and behold, the Egyptians marched after them. So they were very afraid and the children of Israel cried out to the Lord."

Did you catch those five words? ***So they were very afraid.*** As my six-year-old daughter used to put it, "They were really, really, really scared!" So what do you do if you have the heart of a mouse and you are really, really, really scared?

There are three keys in this story to help you face your fear. If you use them, your fear will belong to God, who can handle it. The first is to *stand still and don't run*, the second is to *remember*, and the third is to *go forward*.

STAND STILL AND DON'T RUN

Have you ever had someone jump out at you from behind a bush? Or sneak up on you in the dark? Or scare you for the fun of it? My wife tried to scare me for the fun of it when we were first married. I walked in the apartment one day after taking out the trash. Not seeing my wife, I called out, "Donna?" Silence. And then I heard this blood-curdling "Raaaarh!"

Remember, I had completed basic training with the Air Force. I had been in fights. I had seen it all. So, what did this macho man do? I screamed and RAN as Donna jumped out of the closet, laughing.

Our first impulse when we are scared is to RUN! That is why Moses (in Exodus 14:13) told the children of Israel: "Do not be afraid. Stand still." Moses knew that the sight of the soldiers would bring terror to their hearts, and they would flee. He also knew this was an opportunity to show God's power.

You will never *fly* if you *run* from your fear. You cannot function as God intends for you when you are afraid and, in the darkness, fail to see God's willingness to save you. That is why our first key is **stand still.** Don't run from the light.

Consider this description of the Christian's battle gear as found in Ephesians 6:10-17:

Finally brethren, be strong in the Lord and in the power of His might. Put on the whole armor of God, that you may be able to stand against the wiles of the devil. For we do not wrestle with flesh and blood, but against principalities, against powers, against the rulers of the darkness of this age, against spiritual hosts of wickedness in the heavenly places. Therefore, take up the whole armor of God, that you may be able to withstand in the evil day, and having done all, to stand.

Stand therefore, having girded your waist with truth, having put on the breastplate of righteousness, and having shod your feet with the preparation of the gospel of peace; above all, taking the shield of faith with which you will be able to quench all the fiery darts of the wicked one. And take the helmet of salvation, and the sword of the Spirit, which is the word.

Did you notice what part of the body isn't covered? Every part is protected with one exception — the back! You cannot turn your back on fear and win because *running makes it difficult to trust God.*

When we allow fear to control us, we are like an immigrant man who lived years ago in upstate New York. He began to cross a frozen lake. As he approached the center of the lake, fear overwhelmed him and he dropped to his knees and began to crawl, terrified lest the ice should crack and he would drown. As he crept along, a young man with a team of horses pulling a great load of pig iron drove past him. The immigrant man noticed that the ice supported the team of horses, but he continued to crawl across the lake. He was so blinded by fear that he couldn't believe what he saw.[4] That's how it is when we allow our fears to overwhelm us. We know God is there, but we find it difficult to trust Him. Also, *running will turn your attitude negative.*

Speaking of becoming negative, did you catch what the Israelites did? In Exodus 14:11-12, it says:

Then they said to Moses, "Because there were no graves in Egypt, have you taken us away to die in the wilderness? Why have you so dealt with us, to bring us up out of Egypt? Is this not the word we told you in Egypt, saying, 'Leave us alone that we may serve the Egyptians?' For it would have been better for us to serve the Egyptians than to die in the wilderness."

I'm glad God called Moses, instead of me, to shepherd the Israelites. Every time a crisis came up … every time someone posed a threat … every time they faced a new challenge … every time they were confronted with fear . . the Israelites became negative and didn't trust God with their concerns. Don't you wonder if Moses ever wanted to say, "Enough! I wish you *were* back in Egypt!" Do you wonder how Moses could go on loving and leading them? I believe he knew they were afraid.

I have heard similar negative words from those I have pastored. "We have never done it that way before," or "We don't like all the changes." People have said, "There are too many new faces in our congregation. Pastor, we are growing too fast." Others have even summed up their displeasure with, "We like things the way they used to be." When I hear those kinds of statements, I remind myself that fear is present. Then I can continue to love, because I know fear can make us negative.

Fear also can cause us to make crazy decisions. On August of 1989, *Time* printed a story about a man from East Detroit who died of fear. He had taken a number of fur-trapping expeditions over the years and had been bitten by his share of ticks. Then he heard about Lyme disease, which is carried by deer ticks. He became obsessed with the fear that he had been bitten by an infected tick and had passed the disease on to his wife.

Doctors tested him and assured him he didn't have Lyme disease and that, even if he did, the disease was virtually impossible to transmit to his wife. But the man didn't believe the doctors. Paranoid because of his fear, the man killed his wife and then himself. The police found the man's mailbox jammed with material describing Lyme disease and a slip confirming a doctor's appointment for yet another Lyme disease test.[5]

When we are afraid, our fears take over and we do crazy things. We all know family members and friends who have made crazy decisions — decisions that made no sense. We grab them … shake them … scream at them. "Can't you see? Don't you realize that you are destroying yourself?" And yet, we can't get through to them because they are running from their fear.

REMEMBER AND BE ENCOURAGED

Just as the first key to overcoming fear is to *not run*, the second key to overcoming fear is to **remember**.

Listen to Moses' words in Exodus 14:13 as the Hebrew people were being pursued by the Egyptian soldiers: "Do not be afraid. Stand still, and **see** the salvation of the Lord, which He will accomplish for you today." Moses didn't use the word "remember" — rather, he used the word "see." What did Moses want the people to see?

Imagine that you are standing on the bank of the Red Sea. There are Egyptians behind you, water in front of you. Death by sword on one hand, death by drowning on the other. Great choices: bleeding or gurgling! Is there anything else to see? Yes! In his fear, Moses saw — and remembered — all that God had done for him. Hebrews 11:27 states: "By faith Moses forsook Egypt, not **fearing** the wrath of the king; for he endured as **seeing** Him who is invisible" (bold emphasis mine).

When you are afraid, you must find a way to see — remember

— all that God has done for you in the past. That will enable you to see that which He will accomplish for you today. Seeing and remembering is prevalent throughout Scripture. As the shepherd, David prepared to fight the giant Goliath, and he remembered. Do you recall the story? King Saul tried to give the little boy his armor, and David declined, citing:

> *Your servant used to keep his father's sheep, and when a lion or a bear came and took a lamb out of the flock, I went out after it and struck it, and delivered the lamb from its mouth; and when it arose against me, I caught it by its beard, and struck it and killed it. Your servant has killed both the lion and the bear; and this uncircumcised Philistine will be like one of them, seeing he has defied the armies of the living God. Moreover, David said, The Lord, who delivered me from the paw of the lion and from the paw of the bear, He will deliver me from the hand of this Philistine (1 Samuel 17:37).*

When faced with the biggest challenge of his life, David remembered God, and went from shepherd to soldier. King Saul didn't believe David could defeat Goliath. David's own brothers thought he was crazy. Nobody believed in him. But David remembered his God could overcome things greater than him.

Read the apostle Paul's account of his struggles with the thorn in his flesh. He pleads with the Lord three times to take his pain away. Finally, Jesus speaks to him: "My grace is sufficient for you" (2 Corinthians 12:7-10). Paul accepts his thorn, because now, as he recalls his thorn, he remembers "fourteen years ago ... such a one was caught up to the third heaven" (2 Corinthians 12:2). Paul remembered all that God had done and went from victim to victor.

Accepting thorns? Facing giants? Trapped between roaring

chariots and raging seas? They were people just like us. They overcame fear by remembering all that God had done in the past.

One Sunday morning, during my time in the Air Force in Montana, I walked the aisle of our church. I told the pastor that I felt as if God wanted me to do something special with my life, but I wasn't sure what. He responded, "Tim, if you will tell God that you will do whatever He asks you to do, He will make His wishes known."

I didn't want to tell God that I'd do whatever. I didn't want to leave the door wide open for Him. I had expected my pastor to tell me what to do. Ever felt that way? Being the mature Christian that I was, I pouted and left the church for a few months.

For the next four months, I was miserable. I couldn't sleep. I argued with my friends. I went back to see my pastor. "Tim, if you'll tell God that you will do whatever He asks, He will make His wishes known." *Great!* I thought, *You're no help!*

On a Saturday night in a local movie theater, I began to cry. I knelt down, right there in the theater, and prayed: "Father, I am miserable. If You will make it clear to me … if You'll tell me what to do or who to be … I will do my best."

He said to me, "I want you to preach. Stop running from Me."

The next morning at church, I walked the aisle again. This time I told my pastor what had happened, that God had called me to preach. "That's what I have been waiting to hear," Pastor Grady exclaimed. Then Pastor Grady called my wife down front. I had not shared with Donna what had happened the night before. I'm sure that she knew something was up. When your husband is kneeling and crying in the middle of the movie, something is wrong! When she arrived down front beside me, my pastor said Donna had shared with him several weeks earlier that God had given her a vision. In that vision, I was standing in the pulpit preaching. Pastor Grady had requested that my wife not tell me.

"Preaching had to be your decision," he said, "and this confirms that you made the right one."

That was over thirty years ago. Every time I feel like quitting, every time I get discouraged, every time I want to run, I remember my call and Donna's vision — and I am encouraged to know that I am in God's will.

How about you? What has God done in your life that you can remember as you confront new fears? How many lions ... or tigers ... or bears ... has He given you victory over? How many times has His grace been sufficient for you?

Go Forward and Trust God

Would you like to go from surviving to flying? Are you a victim who would like to be victor? Then you must *not run* from your fear, you must *remember* what God has done, and you must trust God and **go forward!**

The Lord said to Moses, "Why do you cry to me? Tell the children of Israel to go forward" (Exodus 14:15). Going forward is the heart of the story. This is where the rubber meets the road! It does no good to stand still and not run, or to remember and see God, if you are unwilling to go forward.

Going forward does not mean running impulsively. Rather, it means choosing a path, acting in faith, and stepping out. I like what Exodus 14:16 says: "Lift up your rod." Moses did not need to lift up his rod for God to part the sea. Moses needed to lift up his rod so that he could show that he had overcome his fear. He didn't lift the rod so that he could free God to work. He lifted the rod so that he could free himself and move forward.

Sometimes you have to be willing to act by faith. Are you sitting back, holding out on a decision to follow Christ, and waiting for your questions to be answered? Or perhaps you believe God has spoken to you, challenged you to move your life in a different direction. You need to act on faith. Faith means believing even when there are no answers to the questions. Yes, it's that simple. Just choose to trust. Choose to believe that God is working. Choose to believe that He is with you. Choose to believe that God will come through.

I like how the story in Exodus unfolds. "Then Moses stretched out his hand over the sea; and the Lord caused the sea to go back by a strong east wind all that night, and made the sea into dry land, and the waters were divided. So the children of Israel went …" (Exodus 14:21-22a). Isn't that great? God came through, and their fears were overcome. But they first had to *trust* and *move*.

Chuck Swindoll, in his book called *Living Above the Level of Mediocrity*, tells the following story:

> *Legend has it that a man was lost in the desert, just dying for a drink of water. He stumbled upon an old shack — a ramshackle, windowless, roofless, weather-beaten old shack. He looked about this place and found a little shade from the heat of the desert sun. As he glanced around, he saw a pump about fifteen feet away — an old, rusty water pump. He stumbled over to it, grabbed the handle, and began to pump up and down, up and down. Nothing came out.*
>
> *Disappointed, he staggered back. He noticed off to the side an old jug. He looked at it, wiped away the dirt and dust, and read a message that said, "You need to prime the pump with all the water in this jug, my friend. P.S.: Be sure you fill the jug again before you leave."*

He popped the cork out of the jug and sure enough, it was almost full of water! Suddenly, he was faced with a decision. If he drank the water, he could live. Ah, but if he poured all the water in the rusty pump, maybe it would yield fresh, cool water from down deep in the well, all the water he wanted.

He studied the possibilities of both options. What should he do, pour it in the old pump and take a chance on fresh, cool water — or drink what was in the old jug and ignore its message? Should he waste all the water on the hopes of those flimsy instructions written, no telling how long ago?

Reluctantly, he poured all the water into the pump. Then he grabbed the handle and began to pump, squeak, squeak, and squeak. Still nothing came out! Squeak, squeak, and squeak. A little bit began to dribble out, then a small stream, and finally it gushed! To his relief fresh, cool water poured out of the rusty pump. Eagerly, he filled the jug and drank from it. He filled it another time and once again drank from its refreshing contents.

Then he filled the jug for the next traveler. He filled it to the top, popped the cork back on, and added this little note: "Believe me, it really works. You have to give it all away before you can get anything back."[6]

And so it is with overcoming our fears. God's way really works! But you have to be willing to trust — to give it all away — to follow God's instructions written so long ago.

Are you confronted by fear? Afraid of the future? Controlled by the past? Fearful of your enemies? Afraid of your friends? Scared of death? Troubled by life? Do yourself a favor. Try overcoming your fear God's way. **Stand still and don't run. Remember. Go forward.** If you'll use these three keys — God's keys — you will find that you have a tiger's heart, not that of a mouse!

Psalm 51:1-2

Be gracious to me, O God, according to your lovingkindness; According to the greatness of your compassion blot out my transgressions. Wash me thoroughly from my iniquity, And cleanse me of my sin.

4

OOPS! I HAVE FAILED (PART I)

I have never forgotten that horrible day. I just froze. I didn't swing at all. Like the ghost of Captain Cutler in a re-run of Scooby Doo, my personal failure still rises from the abyss to haunt me. I am referring to my Little League All-Stars tournament game. It was a winner-take-all game, with the winner advancing to the State championship tournament. Our team was trailing 8 to 7. The bases were loaded, the count was full and the tension was high!

Just two weeks before, I had faced a similar situation in our regional tournament. The pitch had been right down the middle, I had hit a grand slam home run, and we celebrated a championship! This pitch was right down the middle, too, but I froze. Strike three! Game over. The Mighty Casey — I mean, Timmy — had struck out! To make matters worse, we were the best team. To make matters even "worser" (as my uncle used to say), I had made a couple of errors in the field that had cost us the lead. After the game, I climbed into my momma's car and left for home. I fully intended to NEVER play baseball again … EVER! The season was over, my career was over, summer vacation was almost over, and my desire to try anything was OVER!

It was a devastating moment of failure, and it would not be my last. As a matter of fact, I have experienced the same terrible feeling of failure on multiple occasions since, on bigger occasions than Little League. I imagine you have, too.

Most of us don't fly the first time we try, or the second, and perhaps not the third. It would be easy to succumb to disappointment, to consider ourselves unable to achieve the goal to which we have committed time and energy. But God gives us hope. He doesn't kick us off the team when we fall; rather, He picks us up, dusts us off, and puts the bat back in our hands. We have a faith that gives us hope — even when we fail. Our "how-to book," the Bible, provides three steps to overcoming our failure: recognize it, reverse it, and release it. I want us to deal with the first of the three in this chapter.

Recognize It

The first step to dealing with failure is to **recognize it.** Part of recognizing is admitting that the failure exists. I meet people every day who refuse to admit they have made mistakes. They will not talk about their sin; they will not face their imperfection. They point their fingers, highlighting other people's weaknesses. They tell me every instance where they have been wronged. But they won't admit *their* wrongs. My grandmother used to say that was the "pot calling the kettle black."

I love how the Bible is full of stories about less-than-perfect people like Abraham, David, Rahab, the woman at the well, Peter, and Saul — all individuals who make less-than-ideal choices and still live above-average lives. The Bible is a how-to book on dealing with failure. It is a beautiful testimony on how God deals with our imperfections.

In Psalm 51, we find a perfect lesson on what to do when we recognize our sins. In this psalm, penned by King David after he had committed adultery with Bathsheba and had her husband killed to hide his deed, we find three basic Old Testament words used to describe sin:

> *Have mercy upon me, O God, according to Your lovingkindness;*
> *According to the multitude of Your tender mercies,*
> *Blot out my **transgressions**.*
> *Wash me thoroughly from my **iniquity**,*
> *And cleanse me of my **sin**. (Psalm 51:1-2, bold emphasis mine)*

Although you can find these three words throughout the Bible, they are grouped together here. Together, they offer the best argument, and the best definition, of failure.

David first uses the word "transgression." To transgress means "to break a commandment" or "to disobey an order." It means "to directly disobey God." He says to zig, and we zag. He says to go, and we stay. He says to stay, and we go. He says no, and we say yes. We cross the line and break His principles. We can do this in a number of ways. We cross the line with our mouths when we utter negative words. We cross the line with our actions when we lose our tempers. We cross the line in our apathy and refuse to help a neighbor in need.

The second word David uses is "iniquity." Iniquity occurs when something designed for good is bent and misused for evil purposes. The best illustration of this in our culture is sex. Something God meant for good has been turned into something perverted. But iniquity can occur in many areas. We misuse our time when we spend it selfishly instead of the way God intended. We misuse our possessions when we worship them instead of the God who provided them. We can even misuse our skills and abilities and use them for our benefit rather than God's glory.

Finally, David speaks of "sin." Sin means "to miss the mark." It is an archery word. You shoot at the target but miss. We can miss the mark in our marriages, at our jobs, in school, with our finances, as parents, or as a citizen. You don't have to be a murderer to miss the mark. You don't have to be a thief or be immoral. You just have to be living. All of us have taken our best shots, only to fall short. We missed the mark.

I stopped and considered how many mistakes I make, and the knowledge humbled me. I did some basic math (about the only math that I can do), and my discoveries blew me away.

I suspect most of you are like me. You can look back at the end of a day and see where you failed at least once in these three major areas. I mean, not many days go by that I can't find where I have crossed the line, or misused my time and talents, or been off target at least once.

So, let's return to my math. I took the Bible's statement that the average lifespan is seventy years. I subtracted ten years for childhood, and I multiplied my number of failures per year by sixty. So, if you commit three mistakes a day, that's 1,095 per year. Multiply 1,095 times sixty years, and you will have committed 65,700 errors in your lifetime. That's a lot of sin to answer for on Judgment Day! Those who know me would say that I am a "good" man, but would a good man really commit 65,700 sins? No wonder the Bible says, "There is none righteous, no, not one" (Romans 3:10).

You may be saying, "Tim, I don't commit three offenses per day. I might confess to one." Well, if you make one mistake per day, you not only are better than Tim Coker, but you are a noble person. If you make only one mistake per day, that's 365 mistakes per year (let's forget leap year). If you live to be seventy, you'll answer on Judgment Day for 21,900 failures!

Or you may be thinking, *I don't commit one sin, transgression or iniquity a day. I can admit one a week.* Wow! That's a high standard. I have good news and bad news for you. The good news is that you might be on another level of morality from everyone else on the planet! The bad news is that you will commit fifty-two sins per year, or 3,120 in a lifetime. How many are you allowed before you are considered a sinner, imperfect or flawed?

None!

Do you see where I am going with this? Everyone is flawed. Everyone we work with or live with or play with has failed — and so have you.

There are people who will say they have never practiced iniquity. They have never transgressed the Law. They have never missed the mark. Some of you are those people. There is a word for that: liar. The Bible says: "If we say we have no sin, we deceive ourselves, and the truth is not in us" (1 John 1:8), and "If we say that we have not sinned, we make Him a liar" (1 John 1:10). If you really think you have achieved perfection, or have any doubt about your flaws, I suggest you ask your spouse. (This usually works for me.) Or ask your kids … or your coworkers … or … wouldn't it be easier to simply admit the truth?

Donna and I have been blessed with two wonderful children. They are not perfect, but as children, they were extremely honest. Our son, Christopher, usually told us what was going on in his life. When he was younger, we could count on being told what had happened during the school day. He would share all — the good and the bad. "I got an 'A' on my spelling test" or "I got in trouble at recess," he would say. He was honest. He 'fessed up.

I believe most children start out honest. They'll 'fess up. But over time, they learn to hide their failures. They grow into covering their mistakes.

Imagine you are soaring. A red light flashes in your mind, a warning of a problem ahead. You are in control, you think. You can ignore this warning, you tell yourself. You also ignore the co-pilot sitting right beside you, ready to help. And you keep saying you are in control right up to the moment you crash. We must, as part of our flight training, *unlearn* the tendency to hide our flaws. We must first recognize, and then confess, our failure. Then we are in position to receive God's help regarding our sin.

As I mentioned in the beginning of this chapter, we have a Heavenly Father who picks us up, dusts us off, and puts the bat back in our hands. Recognizing our sin allows Him to pick us up. We do not have to be defined by our failures.

Winston Churchill was one of the key figures of World War II. He, perhaps more than any other leader, was responsible for saving Europe from Nazi domination. His courage, shown in his statement, "We will fight them on the beaches, we will fight them on the ground, we will fight them in the air," is legendary. His resolve and "never give in" attitude still inspires students of history. But Churchill had to overcome failure, too. In fact, had he not faced and overcome his own failure during WWI, he would have missed WWII.

Winston Churchill was already a key military figure — a major decision-maker — during World War I. As Lord of the Admiralty, he devised a major invasion, sending British warships south around the Gallipoli peninsula, hoping to establish a new supply line to Russia. The campaign was a disaster; 56,000 lives were lost. Another 200,000 were wounded, in addition to the equipment and financial loss. Historians still debate whether Churchill received too much of the blame. Was he a scapegoat? Whatever the verdict, some things are certain. Churchill lost his position, his influence and his reputation. He left the British Navy a failure.

Churchill could have stayed down after Gallipoli, but *he got up.* He could have quit, but he refused. He lived to fight another day! He learned to overcome failure, took the proverbial bat back into his hands, and history was altered.

I learned to overcome, too. I lived to play baseball again. I know what it is like to fail, to admit my sin, and be picked up and dusted off by my Father. Have you learned to overcome your failure? Are you ready to try your hand at *flying* again? Then *recognize* your failure for what it is, and take the last two steps toward recovery.

Mark 14:66-72 (NKJV)

Now as Peter was below in the courtyard, one of the servant girls of the high priest came. And when she saw Peter warming himself, she looked at him and said, "You also were with Jesus of Nazareth." But he denied it, saying, "I neither know nor understand what you are saying." And he went out on the porch, and a rooster crowed. And the servant girl saw him again, and began to say to those who stood by, "This is one of them." But he denied it again. And a little later those who stood by said to Peter again, "Surely you are one of them; for you are a Galilean, and your speech shows it." Then he began to curse and swear, "I do not know this man of whom you speak!" A second time the rooster crowed. Then Peter called to mind the word that Jesus had said to him, "Before the rooster crows twice, you will deny Me three times." And when he thought about it, he wept.

5

OOPS! I HAVE FAILED (PART II)

His name is Roy Riegels. He was an All-American football player at Georgia Tech, playing both offense and defense. He was a success, a leader on and off the field, but he is remembered for his failure. Roy Riegels is better known as "Wrong Way" Riegels.[7]

Roy earned his nickname in the 1929 Rose Bowl game. Georgia Tech was playing the University of California at Berkeley. Roy was playing defense for Georgia Tech when someone on the California team fumbled the ball. Roy ran over, scooped it up, and began to race toward the end zone, sixty-five yards away. As he was running, one of his teammates came panting up behind him, yelling, "You're running the wrong way!" The crowd roared and screamed, but Roy couldn't hear. So, his teammate caught him and tackled him. And, from their new position on the five-yard line, California scored.

At halftime, the coach of Tech entered a silent locker room. There, in the midst of a group of college students, sat Roy Riegels — head in his hands, weeping like a baby.

I heard this story on the radio again the other day. How many times since 1929 has it been told? It is a story that refuses to die. Then it dawned on me: We like this story because it hits us where we live.

We all relate to old Wrong Way Riegels, don't we? Most of us have had those moments when we sat there … head in our hands … motionless … weeping like a baby. We meant to run the right way, but we were wrong. We made poor choices. We zigged when we should have zagged. We spoke when we should have remained silent. We remained silent when we should have spoken. We failed!

Every time I hear the Roy Riegels story, I think of the apostle Peter. I love Peter. He is a "wrong way" human if ever there was one. One moment he is walking on water, the next he is scared to death. One moment he is confessing Christ, the next he is denying he ever met Jesus.

Wow! Talk about running the wrong way. Haven't you been there? Haven't we all been there? Haven't you felt like Peter after he denied his Lord and heard the rooster crow? Mark says he "wept" (Mark 14:72). Luke says he "wept bitterly" (Luke 22:62). Just like Wrong Way Riegels, only 1,900 years earlier, Peter knew the sting of failure. The question is, "What did Peter do about it?" The bigger question is, "What will you do about your 'IT'?"

The bottom line of every religion … every belief system … every code … is how it deals with failure. Every belief system expresses wonderful ideals. Every religion describes the perfect life. But what happens when we fail? When we are less than perfect? What do we do when we are below ideal? I have some great news for you! We have a faith that gives us hope, even when we fail. Our how-to book, the Bible, gives us three steps to overcoming our mistakes. Last chapter, we looked at the first step: *Recognize Failure*.

This chapter, let's deal with the last two steps: *Reverse Direction* and *Release Guilt*.

Reverse Direction

The second step in dealing with failure is to **reverse direction** by reversing how we see failure. Most people feel some level of regret over their mistakes; the greater the mistake and/or consequences, the bigger the sense of regret. In fact, I would argue that regret is a healthy, normal response to failure. But regret is not enough; we need to reverse the direction of our thinking, which leads to action (repentance). The scales may indicate that I am overweight and out of shape. I may really regret what the scales indicate, but unless I change my thinking and direction (which usually means time spent at Fitness World and a healthier diet), I will remain overweight and out of shape. You see, God is after more than our regret. He wants us to move from regretting our mistakes to reversing our thinking about our mistakes. The Bible uses the word "repent" to describe this reversal of thinking. After Peter "thought about it," he wept (Mark 14:72).

I went to California a few years ago to a seminar on preaching. The seminar took place at the largest Southern Baptist church in America, Saddleback Community Church in the Los Angeles area. The pastor of the church, Rick Warren, urged us to "preach for repentance" and used a parable to describe the biblical word "repentance." Here is his story:

> *Imagine a speed boat on an open lake, flying along at 70 miles per hour. It is set on autopilot and is heading east. Now, imagine that you have a desire to change the boat's direction. You desire a move toward the west. You pull the levers and fight the steering wheel and slowly turn the boat west. You fight and strain, and grunt and groan, and fight and strain, and grunt and groan, and ... you get the picture. You are at war because the boat's autopilot is set against you. Each time you let go or*

relax, the boat turns in the opposite direction and heads east again.[8]

That's how most people deal with failure. They fight and strain, and grunt and groan to change their behavior. They succeed for a short period of time, but the moment they relax, or stop fighting, they're right back in the same old lifestyle. They make the same old mistakes, and experience the same old guilt. Do they feel remorse? Yes. Are they sorry for what they've done? Of course. Will they try again? Probably. But they'll fail again — and feel just as guilty, and even more frustrated, because they haven't really repented.

Real repentance is changing your autopilot. It is to reverse your thinking about sin. It isn't enough to feel remorse over your mistakes. You must desire a new direction and make the choice to change. You will still mess up. You will still have times of failure. You will still have moments of sin. But you will not have the exhausting struggle that comes from trying to live a false life, a life where inner desires of going east do not match the outward actions of wanting to head west.

Flying, just as in the scenario above, includes an autopilot function. Autopilot allows you to function in that normal part of life without thought. You simply go with the flow you have preset in your life. But autopilot is only good if the direction you set is the right one. You see, only Christ can help reverse your inner desires. Only He can change your autopilot so that your attitudes and actions move in the same direction. When you reach that point, you will be able to soar in the clouds with contentment, knowing you are in God's flight plan.

You no longer have to live with frustration for your past failures. You *can* begin again and head in a new direction. Have you made a decision that you want your life to head in the direction of Christ? Ask God to help you *reverse your thinking* and change your autopilot.

Release It

Once you have *recognized your sin* and *reversed your direction*, the final step to overcoming the failure that keeps you from flying is to **release your guilt**. The fantastic news about our Lord and Savior is His wonderful ability to free us from the guilt of past sin, the guilt that steals the air that lifts our wings and keeps us from enjoying the life God intends for us. But that's not all. He changes us into His instruments: from sinners to servants! That is why Peter's story does not end in Mark 14 with Peter's denial of Jesus. As far as he was concerned, there would be no more visions … no more miracles … no more fishers of men. It was OVER! But God's kingdom never stops because of failure. God moves us from withdrawal to winning, from hiding to hallelujah, and from failure to fishing!

On the day that Jesus rose from the dead, an angel greeted the women at the tomb with these words: "Do not be alarmed. You seek Jesus of Nazareth, who was crucified. He is risen! He is not here! See the place where they laid Him. But go, tell His disciples — **and Peter** — that He is going before you into Galilee; there you will see Him, as He said to you" (Mark 16:6-7). Did you catch those two little words "and Peter"? "And Peter" makes the release of guilt possible. "And Peter" explains the change in Peter's life. Peter was freed from his guilt and soared. He spent the rest of his life telling others about it.

Peter felt guilt over denying Christ. He could have chosen to avoid Christ. He could have chosen not to accept His forgiveness. He could have stayed in the proverbial locker room with Wrong Way Riegels, head buried in shame, never dealing with his failure. But he did what we must do. He released his guilt.

Too many of us spend our lives lamenting mistakes of the past. If God Himself is willing to "remember our sins no more" (Hebrews 8:12), then shouldn't we release ourselves from the burden of all that guilt? Isn't it time for us guilty sinners to drop the baggage of past mistakes or hurts and become forgiven servants, to feel the power of God lift us to new horizons?

So, let's get back to our story about Wrong Way Roy Riegels. Halftime came, and the coach stood before his players. He boldly proclaimed, "Same team that started the first half will start the second." Roy sat there, speechless. He couldn't believe it, after what he had done. He mustered the courage to speak: "But, Coach —"

The coach interrupted his words: "Roy, get up and go back out there — the game is only half over."[9]

I bet those 3,000 people who heard Peter's sermon at Pentecost are glad he released his guilt (Acts 2:1-41). Every time I read 1 or 2 Peter, I am glad that he played the "second half" of his life!

There's the rest of your life to play! There are skies to soar and wonderful experiences God has created for you. But you cannot enjoy them unless you give up your guilt.

How about it? Are you still beating yourself up over mistakes and sins of the past? *Realize* your failures, *recognize* your hope in Christ, and *release* your guilt. Get busy serving Him!

PART TWO

Dealing with External Things that Prevent You from Flying

Matthew 18:21-35

Then Peter came and said to Him, "Lord, how often shall my brother sin against me and I forgive him? Up to seven times?" Jesus said to him, "I do not say to you, up to seven times, but up to seventy times seven. "For this reason the kingdom of heaven may be compared to a king who wished to settle accounts with his slaves. When he had begun to settle them, one who owed him ten thousand talents was brought to him. But since he did not have the means to repay, his lord commanded him to be sold, along with his wife and children and all that he had, and repayment to be made. So the slave fell to the ground and prostrated himself before him, saying, 'Have patience with me and I will repay you everything.' And the lord of that slave felt compassion and released him and forgave him the debt. But that slave went out and found one of his fellow slaves who owed him a hundred denarii; and he seized him and began to choke him, saying, 'Pay back what you owe.' So his fellow slave fell to the ground and began to plead with him, saying, 'Have patience with me and I will repay you.' But he was unwilling and went and threw him in prison until he should pay back what was owed. So when his fellow slaves saw what had happened, they were deeply grieved and came and reported to their lord all that had happened. Then summoning him, his lord said to him, 'You wicked slave, I forgave you all that debt because you pleaded with me. Should you not also have had mercy on your fellow slave, in the same way that I had mercy on you?' And his lord, moved with anger, handed him over to the torturers until he should repay all that was owed him. My Heavenly Father will also do the same to you, if each of you does not forgive his brother from your heart.

6

LEARNING TO FORGIVE

I have spent the first part of this book dealing with "internals." We have discussed how adjusting your thinking about God, your failures and fears, and your inner attitudes enable you to soar. Learning to fly, however, must also include some "externals." Your flight training needs to impact every area of life — what happens on Monday, as well as what you do on Sunday. For the remaining chapters, I want to look at what God says about daily life. Real life. Life lived in the trenches. Life that includes marriage, parenting, difficulty, growth and disappointment. You'll see that God really knows what He's talking about, and because of this you can learn to fly! Let's begin by discussing **forgiving others**.

Let's face it. There are some things in our lives that are more difficult to deal with than others. I am not necessarily talking about big things, like swimming the English Channel or going to war or losing twenty pounds. I'm talking about the daily, little things that continuously hold us down. Things like schedules, or grocery lists, or bills, or losing twenty pounds (guess what I'm dealing with). These little struggles will turn into big problems if we are not careful, and they will keep us grounded when we want to be flying.

I have been a pastor for thirty years; during this time, I have often wondered about the most difficult thing that God asks us to do. Once, I surveyed our congregation and asked this very question. Naturally, the answers varied. A few claimed giving is the most difficult, while others said witnessing. Still, some stated praying and matters of spiritual discipline are the most difficult. The longer I live and pastor, the more I believe the hardest thing for a follower of Christ to do is to **forgive**.

What should you do when someone fails you? How should you respond when you have been hurt? You most likely have felt mind-melting pain when someone hurt you. You may have experienced exploding anger after being wounded, or know the inner anxiety that accompanies a chance encounter with the offender. The transgression may be a present wound, or it may be decades old. Perhaps an emotional scab has formed, only to be scraped off at an inopportune time.

Harboring inequities weighs us down and keeps us from flying. Our "flight manual," the Bible, helps us deal with past bruises and present wounds. If you struggle to forgive, there are two questions you need to answer: Why should I forgive, and how do I go about doing it?

Why Should I Forgive?

Jesus speaks strongly on the subject of forgiveness when he replies "seventy times seven" in response to Peter's question: "How many times should I forgive my brother?" On another occasion, Jesus says: "For if you forgive others for their transgressions, your Heavenly Father will also forgive you. But if you do not forgive others, then your Father will not forgive your transgressions" (Matthew 6:14-15).

Talk about straightforward! Why does Jesus want us to forgive others? Does this include our spouse? Our parents? Yes, and I find three reasons in this scripture to forgive.

We Should Forgive Because God Forgives

The first reason we need to forgive is **because God forgives us.**

Jesus knows the concept of forgiveness is hard to understand, so He uses a parable to help us understand. In this parable, there are two encounters, two debts, two choices made, and two results. In the first encounter, there is a slave who owes his master 10,000 talents. When he cannot pay, the master to whom the money is owed forgives the debt. This first encounter depicts our relationship with God. He is the Master. We are the slaves. Because of our sin, we owe an insurmountable debt — 10,000 talents. A talent during Jesus' time was worth approximately fifteen years' salary. In our day, the debt would be about $2.34 billion, based on a minimum wage of $7.50/hour. When it comes to failing Him, I am the chief of sinners! Yet, the Master (God) forgives the slave (me). The debt is wiped out. The cost is paid.

The second encounter describes our relationships with those around us. This same servant, who was just forgiven a debt of 10,000 talents, goes to a man who owes him 100 denarii. A denarius was a common man's daily wage. So, in our day, the second man owes about $6,000, also based on $7.50 an hour. The second man cannot repay his debt. Even though the first slave has been forgiven a much greater amount, he refuses to forgive the debt of another. The point of the parable is clear: We cannot out-forgive God! Our sins against God far outweigh the times we have been wronged by others.

You may be thinking: *Wait a minute, Tim, you don't know what I've been through!* I am not saying, nor is Jesus, that the stones thrown at you do not hurt, or haven't created scars. Jesus is telling us *our* sin has caused *Him* scars — and hurt — on a level we cannot fully comprehend. If we trust a Lord who has forgiven us so great a debt, should we not trust Him by forgiving others — even if the debt is greater than $6,000?

WE SHOULD FORGIVE BECAUSE FORGIVING BRINGS FREEDOM

In addition to forgiving because God forgives, **forgiving brings freedom.** You need to forgive as badly as others need to be forgiven. Someone once told me, "Holding a grudge always hurts the one holding it." Although I don't remember who said it, I do know that it has proven to be true. Holding a grudge always hurts the one holding it.

I am reminded of Charles Dickens' character in *Great Expectations*, Miss Havisham, who could not move beyond being jilted on her wedding day. Wikipedia sums her up like this:

> *Humiliated and heartbroken, Miss Havisham suffered a mental breakdown and remained alone in her mansion — never removing her wedding dress, wearing only one shoe, leaving the wedding cake uneaten on the table, and allowing only a few people to see her. She even had the clocks stopped at 20 minutes to 9, the exact time she had received the rejection letter from her fiancé.*[10]

Like Miss Havisham, who could not move beyond being jilted on her wedding day, a lack of forgiveness can choke your freedom and keep you stagnated. Your clock, like Miss Havisham's, might be stuck at 8:40. I have seen grown men cry like babies in my study, still trying to get beyond the "absent father wound" from their childhood.

Lack of forgiveness is why some couples do not trust, why some neighbors do not share, and why many Christians do not love. So, I repeat, Jesus knows what we need to learn: We need to forgive as badly as they need to be forgiven.

We Should Forgive Because God Tells Us To

Third, **we forgive because God tells us to.** This doesn't sound overly compelling, and it certainly doesn't smack of intellectualism, but it is true. Sometimes my choices in life are matters of obedience. I trust Him to know what is best for me, so I choose His model for living. I make choices in all areas of my life: how I treat my wife and children, how I spend my money, how I treat the waitress at Cracker Barrel. My choices reflect my faith, and forgiveness is one of those choices. William Arthur Ward, in *Thoughts of a Christian Optimist* (1968), once said, "We are most like beasts when we kill. We are most like men when we judge. We are most like God when we forgive."[11]

How Do I Forgive?

We have addressed the *why* of forgiveness. The second question we need to address is: How do I forgive? If forgiveness is a matter of choice, and after I have made the choice, where do I begin? Though no one chapter can completely contain all that needs to be said, I can point you in the right direction. Simply put, I can give you three words: *Talk*, *Balk* and *Walk*.

Talk

First, you must **talk.** "To whom should I talk?" you ask. First, I suggest you talk to God. Debrief your life with Him; He is waiting to hear. Tell Him everything. Tell Him how you have been hurt, how you have been wronged, how you feel, how long you have been dealing with IT. Tell your Father everything!

There is a great example of this in Psalm 139, where King David debriefs his innermost thoughts to his Lord. Within this psalm, David shares the good, the bad and the ugly with God.

The good:
> *For You formed my inward parts; You wove me in my mother's womb. I will give thanks to You, for I am fearfully and wonderfully made; Wonderful are Your works, and my soul knows it very well (Psalm 139:13-14).*

The bad:
> *Search me and know my heart; Try me and know my anxious thoughts; And see if there be any hurtful way in me, and lead me in the everlasting way (Psalm 139:23-24).*

The ugly:
> *Do I not hate those who hate You, O Lord? And do I not loathe those who rise up against You? I hate them with the utmost hatred; They have become my enemies (Psalm 139:21-22).*

Wow! Talk about telling God everything. *You mean, the King of Israel — Israel's greatest King — felt hatred?* Yes, he felt hatred … and fear … and guilt … and all the emotions you and I deal with in our lives. David learned to "take it to the Lord in prayer," as an old hymn suggests.

On a side note, David was the best example of a loving king in the Old Testament. On more than one occasion, David had the opportunity to destroy an enemy who longed to kill him, and he responded in grace. It is my belief that his intimacy with God enabled him to process his life, even share his raw emotions, and respond the right way publicly.

After talking with God, you might need to express your thoughts to a professional counselor. I know, we have negative thoughts when we hear *that* word — *counselor!* But the Bible seems to think it's okay to get help from those who are wise. "The way of a fool is right in his own eyes, but a wise man listens to counsel" (Proverbs 12:15). Maybe you don't need a professional counselor to help you deal with your wounds. Then again, maybe you do. If you are having trouble letting go of your enemies, it would be to your advantage to talk with someone skilled at listening.

Last, I would encourage you to talk to yourself. Find an encouraging verse or phrase that will fit your situation and repeat it as often as you need throughout the day.

Years ago, while going through a really difficult time of opposition, I opened my Bible to find a verse Donna had left for me: "Whenever I am afraid, I will put my trust in You" (Psalm 56:3). Over the years, I have uttered that little verse of scripture at least a thousand times, whenever I feel the tug of fear around my spirit.

Oh, yes, I talk to myself! So should you!

Balk

After you have talked, you need to learn to **balk**. By "balk," I am referring to resisting the urge to bring the hurt back, over and over again, so that it stays in your mind. When this pain is present, it chokes out your ability to enjoy the good things around you, including your friends, family and fun!

Some people live their lives wallowing in past hurt. I know people who refuse to attend our church because of something that happened before I became pastor. I have been pastor here for over twenty years. That's over two decades! I know people who have isolated themselves from many of their friends and families, who have burned bridges on their jobs, and who live their lives in "unhappiness mode" simply because they cannot learn to balk. By the way, the inability to balk will also destroy a marriage and other close relationships.

Walk

We can *talk,* and we can *balk.* And finally, we need to learn to **walk.** Our forgiveness must lead to action. There are too many individual circumstances for this chapter to be specific enough for all situations. Let me say, however, true biblical forgiveness leads to some kind of action. I know men and women who have written letters to their deceased parents, both expressing their hurt and putting aside their grudges. I have helped couples renew their marriage vows, willing to face a new future together. I have even read about people who literally bury the hatchet, or bury some other item, as a symbol of moving from a past of pain to a future of promise. I have a friend who wrote out a stack of IOUs from customers at his business and then burned them.

Do you have any hatchets you need to bury? Or an IOU (or ten) that you need to burn, letters you need to write, phone calls you need to make? As psychologist Jerome Bruner once said, "You're more likely to act yourself into feeling than feel yourself into action."[12]

So act! Whatever it is you know you should do, do it. It won't be easy. It takes time to fully recover from old wounds. You'll need the help of your Lord. But please give it a try. You will find new freedom. Maybe you'll soar again!

Genesis 2:23-24

The man said,
"This is now bone of my bones,
And flesh of my flesh;
She shall be called Woman,
Because she was taken out of Man."
"For this reason a man shall leave his father and his mother,
And be joined to his wife; and they shall become one flesh."

7

A Marriage That Gets It

Marriage … Marriage … Marriage! Is there any subject that sparks as much enthusiasm as marriage? I've sat with many young couples and planned enough wedding ceremonies to have learned that few things match the prospect of "Prince Charming and Sleeping Beauty" falling in love and "living happily ever after."

Marriage … Marriage … Marriage! Is there anything more painful than a marriage gone wrong? It's painful for everyone when friends divorce. We all know of unhappy situations where "Prince" isn't so charming and there is no "Beauty," where people are hurt, children are scarred for life, and there is no "happily ever after."

Marriage … Marriage … Marriage! How do you do it right? How do you fly within your marriage?

Consider the first marriage. The Book of Genesis tells us God created the universe, as well as the earth. It tells of His design and purpose for humanity, and it tells of His creation of marriage. So, if you want to understand what it means to have a marriage that "flies," you need to seek help from the Designer.

Glue

A marriage that flies will be based on permanence. That's what the word "joined" means in Genesis 2:24. It means to be stuck together or **glued**. God intends for marriage to be one man plus one woman for life.

I know that I am a little more open-minded when it comes to divorce. In fact, some of my colleagues say that I'm too liberal on this issue. I don't think so. I believe it is possible for a divorced man or woman to have a second chance. I believe a divorced man or woman can still be happy. In fact, I believe it is possible for a divorced man or woman to serve as a leader in the church.

However, divorce was never God's plan, and is only condoned in scripture in a couple of instances (Matthew 19:9; 1 Corinthians 7:10-15). God never intended for us to walk away from marriage the way many seem to be doing today. Quitting is not one of His options. In fact, scripture tells us that God hates divorce. God's picture of marriage has always been "for better, for worse … for richer, for poorer … till death do us part." Why? Because He "glued" us together.

You may be thinking, *I have no problem with what you are saying, Tim. I certainly feel STUCK in my marriage!* If I am describing you, I want you to remember one word — MORE. God intended more for you when He first brought you and your spouse together, and He believes you two can grow more happiness. His dream is for you, as a pair, to see just how thrilling being glued together in marriage can be!

It is this call to permanence in marriage that drives many ministers to include a Charge to the Couple in the wedding ceremonies. One of my favorite charges is the following:

> *Do you promise, in the presence of God and this gathering of family and friends, to seek to be all Christ wants you to be, to*

encourage your husband/wife in his/her spiritual walk?
Do you promise to practice love more as a giver than as a taker?
Do you promise to dedicate your home to the glory of God?
And do you promise to commit your best in making every part of your life together pleasing and honoring to the Lord?[13]

There is something wonderful about saying to the one you love, "I'm not going anywhere. I am in this relationship for life." There is an inner strength that comes from this shared commitment, and a depth of relationship that results from being "glued together."

EMOTION

If the first characteristic of a marriage that flies is glue, the second characteristic is **emotion.** In other words, husbands and wives should love each other. When I use the word love, men and women tend to hear (and think) different things. Men tend to think Song of Solomon 4, where romance, passion and lovemaking dominate the evenings. Women tend to think of a 1 Peter 3 type of love, where husbands give understanding and honor. They imagine late night conversations, where men *really listen* to them. At least some of the time, women want dates and romantic walks, and nice restaurants. I know I am speaking in general terms, but you get the idea. As someone said, "Men spell love S-E-X, and women spell it T-A-L-K."

So who's right? What is supposed to happen: sex or talking? The answer is … BOTH! Both elements are part of God's design for the special union that is marriage, *with emphasis given to our spouse's needs first.*

One of the major problems in today's culture is overstating the importance of romance and passion in marriage. Young couples grow up under the delusion that every night will be a soap opera, where Victor and Nikki finally express their true love for each other. When "real life" moves in, frustration unpacks along with it. Let's face it, Hollywood's picture of romance is a delusion.

Just as wrong as overstating the role of passion, some believe that God isn't into romantic love. Based on this delusion, the world thinks Christians are out of touch because they support sexual abstinence before marriage. The world believes Christians cannot understand the "real problems," such as sexual desire.

So what does God think? I believe God is into romantic love. I believe:

God is into heart-pounding, pulse-racing, palm-sweating, dry-mouthed, stomach-churning, old-fashioned ROMANCE!

I remember the first time I put these words on the screen during our worship service. I was teaching our text, in particular Genesis 2:23, where Adam is presented with Eve and he proclaims: "This is now bone of my bones, flesh of my flesh; she shall be called Woman, because she was taken out of Man." I shared that Adam wasn't uttering theology (though there is a tremendous amount of theology in what he said), he was proclaiming joy. He was saying, "Wow! My life has been missing something. And that something is you. And that something is GOOD!"

I sensed some people were uncomfortable with the notion of romance being mentioned from the pulpit. My question was, and still is, "Why?" Did not our Heavenly Father give us the gift of romance? Has He not planted in us a desire and attraction for the opposite gender? Does He not give us both guidelines and permission in His Word, so that we might enjoy and celebrate this gift?

As I write these words, I am approaching my wedding anniversary. Next month, Donna and I will celebrate almost four decades together! We have had both good and bad times. I suspect our romance has not always met Hollywood's expectations, but I still feel heart-pounding, stomach-churning love for her. And God is pleased! A marriage that "flies" makes room for emotion.

Tension

We have covered glue and emotion. The third ingredient of a marriage that "flies" is **tension**. I can hear some of you shouting, "Tension? That's all we have in our house — tension!"

Not that kind of tension! I'm talking about the tension that exists between the old and new. Genesis 2:24 states: "For this reason, a man shall leave his father and mother, and be joined to his wife; and the two shall become one flesh.' You cannot have two things joined together to become something new without change — and, as we know, change causes tension.

Don't think that God is calling us to disconnect from our mothers and fathers. "A man shall leave his father and mother" is not a statement of geography, but rather a declaration of priority. When we choose a partner for life, in effect we are saying, "You are more important than any other earthly relationship." Earthly relationships include our in-laws, coworkers, friends, hobbies and possessions.

When Donna and I were newlyweds, I worked second shift at a textile mill (4:00 p.m. until 12:00 a.m.). I remember coming home around 1:00 a.m. and thought, since everyone is asleep, and since I needed some time to wind down after a hard day's work, I'd play some basketball in the yard before going to bed. I didn't consider that Donna might have stayed up, waiting for me to come home. Can you see this picture? I am outside shooting basketball at one o'clock in the morning, while my wife waits inside to see her husband. Talk about tension when I finally made my way inside!

After dealing with her disappointment ... and apologizing ... and explaining my reasoning ... and apologizing, I decided to take the advice of the Sesame Street gang from years ago when they told Ernie, "You have to put down the ducky if you want to play the saxophone." In other words, I had to say *no* to something good in order to say *yes* to something better.

I believe God wants us to say no to some good things/relationships in order to say yes to something better.

There is a great temptation to believe that one can be married and still act single. There is a phrase for this: IT WON'T WORK! Some wonderful young couples have wound up hurt, disillusioned or divorced because one or both could not leave the old habits for the new way of life. Husbands and wives must, and should, deal with this tension. Simply put, as my mom used to say: If you're married, you're married.

Sanctification

Our marriages are now *glued*, full of *emotion*, and *tension-resolving*. Finally, a marriage that "flies" will be a **sanctified** marriage. The word sanctification sounds scary. Sanctification has become a controversial word in Christian circles, and an unknown commodity in the non-Christian world. God never meant for it to be difficult.

Sanctification means "to be set apart for another use" — in particular, for God's use in His plan. That sounds so theological, doesn't it? It is not only theological; it is also practical. When I think of sanctification, I think of walking with Him through life, including Him in every area of my journey, serving Him and experiencing His best. This includes my marriage. Consider these verses from John 2:

A Marriage That Gets It 79

On the third day there was a wedding in Cana of Galilee, and the mother of Jesus was there. Now both Jesus and His disciples were invited to the wedding. And when they ran out of wine, the mother of Jesus said to Him, "They have no more wine." Jesus said to her, "Woman, what does your concern have to do with me? My hour has not yet come." His mother said to the servants, "Whatever He says to you, do it." Now there were six waterpots of stone, according to the manner of purification of the Jews, containing twenty or thirty gallons apiece. Jesus said to them, "Fill the water pots with water." And they filled them up to the brim. And He said to them, "Draw some out now, and take it to the master of the feast." And they took it. When the master of the feast had tasted the water that was made wine, and did not know where it came from (but the servants who had drawn the water knew), the master of the feast called the bridegroom. And he said to him, "Every man at the beginning sets out the good wine, and when the guests have well drunk, then the inferior. You have kept the good wine until now!" This beginning of signs Jesus did in Cana of Galilee, and manifested His glory; and His disciples believed in Him. (John 2:1-11)

During one of my seminary courses, we did an interesting exercise using the above passage. The professor asked us to write down any great thought or truth that came to mind as we read the miracle at Cana. I thought this assignment was EASY ... I mean, this was Cana ... water into wine. I jotted down a few thoughts. My classmates did the same. We were ready when the teacher asked for our findings. Students immediately began sharing their thoughts. Even though many deep truths were discussed, I observed my professor getting a little perturbed. Finally, in the middle of our intense discussion, he shouted, "You're missing the greatest truth in the passage!" As we sat there bewildered, he continued, "If you want to experience a water-into-wine type miracle in your house, **you had better invite Jesus, and then do what He says!**"

I have never forgotten his words; they form the basis of a sanctified marriage. We must invite the Lord into our homes (marriages) and do what He says. It is not always easy. It requires a big commitment, and it is a lifelong process. A marriage that is set apart will lead to experiencing marriage the way it was designed.

I must confess, I am no Prince Charming. I am not even close. I must also part with a secret: Donna is not Sleeping Beauty. We are not even Victor and Nikki! But we believe we have a marriage that "gets it" and are "flying" toward "happily ever after." So can you!

Deuteronomy 6:4-9

"Hear, O Israel! The Lord is our God, the Lord is one! You shall love the Lord your God with all your heart and with all your soul and with all your might. These words, which I am commanding you today, shall be on your heart. You shall teach them diligently to your sons and shall talk of them when you sit in your house and when you walk by the way and when you lie down and when you rise up. You shall bind them as a sign on your hand and they shall be as frontals on your forehead. You shall write them on the doorposts of your house and on your gates."

8

Then Comes Baby in a Baby Carriage

You cannot fly if your offspring are not in the plane with you. You cannot soar while leaving responsibilities untethered.

You remember the children's rhyme, don't you? "Timmy and Donna sitting in a tree, K-I-S-S-I-N-G. First comes love, then comes marriage … then comes baby in a baby carriage!"

I don't know why that rhyme used to irritate me so much, but it did. Every time I expressed interest in a girl, my friends and classmates would show up, serenading me. The first time I entered into a major relationship, there my friends were: "Then comes Beth with a baby carriage!" Those taunting voices always arrived in time to ruin my day. Finally, when I was in fifth grade and the girl with the carriage was named Crystal, Mrs. McAuliffe (our fifth grade teacher) had enough. "It's time to stop picking on each other, boys and girls. You are becoming young gentlemen and ladies. Besides, a baby changes everything."

As I write the above words (some with tongue in cheek), a well-known athlete is in the news, charged with "criminal domestic violence" against his young son. The man claims he was practicing discipline and calls the tree switch he used a tool of correction. The prosecutor claims he abused the lad and refers to the branch as a weapon. The community I live in is fairly divided in their opinions. Which perspective is correct? Is there a balance? Do we, as Christ's followers, have any insight? What does it take to rear children? What does Crystal … Donna … Timmy … or whoever it is with the baby carriage really need? On what should parents really focus? Remember, after all, a baby changes *everything*. In our scripture at the beginning of this chapter, I believe there is considerable insight from God about what it takes to parent.

Time

First, parenting takes an investment of **time**. I see no way of getting around this issue. In fact, let me give you a rather simple, insignificant, but profound statement. Here it is: You cannot parent without parenting! My fifth grade teacher, Mrs. McAuliffe, was right! When "baby comes in the baby carriage," everything in life changes.

In the previous chapter on marriage, I mentioned the temptation of some young adults to marry while still pursuing the single life. Another misconception that exists in our culture is that we can somehow get maximum results as parents while giving minimum effort. We use phrases such as "quality time" as opposed to "quantity time." I understand the concept, but wonder how do you ensure that time spent with your little ones is quality? I am not sure we can control when those "quality" moments occur.

My experience has been the opposite. It is not quality time vs. quantity time, but rather quantity time leads to quality time. Those special moments of blessing (quality time) are discovered in the midst of many moments spent together (quantity time). In Deuteronomy 6, the writer speaks of quantity time: "Teaching them to your sons (and daughters) as you sit in your house and when you walk by the way and when you lie down and when you rise up."

Parenting takes much time, but even more importantly, much energy. I need to periodically check the amount of time I spend with my family; I must also steward my energy, so they receive my best!

Toughness / Tenderness

Second, good parents must institute both **toughness** and **tenderness** in children's lives. The athlete I mentioned at the beginning of this chapter is being scrutinized not only by authorities, but also in the court of public opinion. It seems as if the world is divided into two groups, either pro-spank or anti-spank, and young mommies and daddies must choose between the two.

In the church where I pastor, both sides are represented. Both groups can support their position from the Bible. "Spare the rod and spoil the child," one side spouts from the many verses in Proverbs dealing with discipline. "Fathers, do not provoke your children to anger," the other side cites from Ephesians 6:4. Who's right? Which side wins? What does the Lord really want?

To put God's wishes in one word, He desires *balance*. We need a balance between toughness and tenderness, and the discernment to know which one is needed in any given moment. Martin Luther said: "'Spare the rod and spoil the child' — that is true; but beside the rod, keep an apple to give him when he has done well."[14]

Is it possible to find this kind of balance? I think it is. In fact, I grew up in a fairly balanced home. Being the only Coker grandson, I was spoiled and nurtured by aunts, uncles, and my grandmother. But I earned, and experienced, my share of discipline. My mother was the primary disciplinarian in our home, and she **excelled** in that role. I have been disciplined with a tree switch, spanked with a belt, paddled, and placed on restriction many times in my life. Not once did I feel abused or unloved. My mother and father were far from perfect, but did the best they could to strike a balance between love and discipline.

Finding the proper balance between tenderness and toughness is more difficult today than in the era when I grew up. Young parents must, however, find a way to incorporate both elements of God's plan into their children's lives. Little ones will struggle with future challenges when there has been no discipline or structure in their daily lives. Conversely, we scar them emotionally and set them up to fail in their relationships when we do not show them true love.

Truth

Just as children require our time and a balance between toughness and tenderness, they also need to learn the **truth**. Remember the words from Deuteronomy 6: "These words which I am commanding you today shall be on your heart. You shall teach them diligently to your sons and shall talk of them …"

There is a line from the Christmas special, *Rudolph the Red-Nosed Reindeer* (which, incidentally, celebrated its fiftieth anniversary in 2017) that I especially like. While most people listen to the wonderful music of Burl Ives, I am intrigued with the lines: "Donner taught Rudolph the 'ins and outs' of being a reindeer. But mostly, he taught him how to avoid the Abominable Snow Monster of the North. He's mean, he's nasty, and he hates everything to do with Christmas." I don't know what the "ins and outs of being a reindeer" are, but Donner did his best to teach them to his young son. Though I am not exactly sure of all the ins and outs of being a human being, I am fairly certain it is our responsibility to teach our little ones (both does and bucks) the truth that we do understand.

As parents, we must teach our children how to live. This teaching will occur in both our spoken word and in our actions. Remember the old phrase: "Most of what your kids learn from you will be caught, not taught." Those are both humbling and true words. I shudder to think of the times I failed to demonstrate on Monday what I shared from the pulpit on Sunday, and have always been grateful that Christopher and Ashton practiced grace!

Children need a model. Fathers, we need to model what it means to be a man for our sons, and show our daughters how a man should treat a lady. Mothers, you need to model what it means to be a woman of God.

I say it again: Children need a model. We must show them love, while telling them of our love. We must teach manners, having shown them manners. Children learn our values by watching us live and hearing us speak. In other words, truth is **both** caught and taught!

As much as we want to protect our children, wise parents will also teach their children how to avoid the pitfalls of life. Again, remember the words of Sam the Snowman: "But mostly, he taught him how to avoid the Abominable Snow Monster of the North." (I never thought I would be using him as a type of Satan, but here we go!) If we as parents (and especially dads) don't teach our children how to avoid the enemy, we may reap devastating consequences.

Trust

Finally, after all our efforts to model, discipline, teach, nurture and love, parents have to **trust** God with the results. After all, He is the one who controls both blessing and cursing. In Deuteronomy 6, He says you should "listen and be careful to do it (keep the Commandments), that it may be well with you and that you may multiply greatly." In other words, we do the best job we can as parents (with God's help) and trust Him with the results.

When I was in sixth grade, my father retired from the Coast Guard. We moved from New York City to Olanta, South Carolina ... talk about moving from city to country! Our family built a house three miles outside of Olanta, and my parents began the ritual of planting a garden. The process was a simple one: On Good Friday, we as a family would plant our entire garden. When it was time to plant the small, spindly tomatoes, my father would use a hoe to dig holes approximately twelve inches apart. He would dig the holes for an entire row, each row about fifty yards in length. Mama would follow Daddy's digging, dropping a tomato plant in every hole. Then someone would follow with a bucket of water and the Dixie cup, dispensing a cup full of water in each hole (and on each plant). That someone was me! After the watering was done, someone from our family would follow and cover up the roots of each plant.

My job, for the next several weeks, was to water those tomato plants every evening. I mean *every evening* (unless it rained). I dreaded that job. For one thing, the garden was located across the street from our house, so I had to carry buckets of water from the faucet to the garden. For another, I always spilled some on my tennis shoes ... or white socks ... or the driveway ... or somewhere. It seemed as if very little of the water made it to the plants. But mostly my frustration came from an inability to see results. It seemed as if nothing was happening. Day after day, I watered those plants, and nothing happened. Then, suddenly, there they were — little green orbs! Within a few more weeks, we had fresh tomatoes. I didn't fully understand it, but all of the effort (along with heat, sunshine and insecticide) paid off.

Parenting is like growing tomatoes. For those of you uncomfortable with that image, remember Jesus' words: "The kingdom of God is like a man who cast seeds upon the soil; and he goes to bed at night and gets up by day, and the seed sprouts and grows — how, he himself does not know" (Mark 4:26-27). We are diligent to invest our time and energy, while both nurturing and training, in our best efforts to pass on the values we treasure.

Most of us, as parents, feel like we spill a lot of water. But we keep working on it, learning from our mistakes, loving and listening as we go, and knowing God is able to come alongside us and turn our best efforts into something wonderful. If we can trust Him to grow tomatoes, we can trust Him to help us with our little ones. After all, He knows little Johnny or Susie or Billy or whoever is in the baby carriage — and He is love!

Acts 16:6-10

They passed through the Phrygian and Galatian region, having been forbidden by the Holy Spirit to speak the word in Asia; and after they came to Mysia, they were trying to go into Bithynia, and the Spirit of Jesus did not permit them; and passing by Mysia, they came down to Troas. A vision appeared to Paul in the night: a man of Macedonia was standing and appealing to him, and saying, "Come over to Macedonia and help us." When he had seen the vision, immediately we sought to go into Macedonia, concluding that God had called us to preach the gospel to them.

9

WHEN I DON'T GET WHAT I WANT

"TODAY'S GAME IS SOLD OUT." Those words were plastered on a huge sign just outside Gate # 4 at Shea Stadium. To a kid in the fourth grade, the boldness of the letters literally screamed, **"There will be no baseball game for Timmy Coker today! No hot dog. No crowd. No peanuts. No Cracker Jacks. No Mets helmet!"**

You see, it was Helmet Day at Shea Stadium, and the first 10,000 kids entering the stadium would receive a free Mets helmet. I packed my baseball glove. I put on my Mets shirt. I put on my Mets baseball hat. My dad put on his Mets straw hat (yes, it was ugly … but it was him). We climbed into the old Bel Air. We crossed the Brooklyn Bridge. We hit the JFK Expressway heading towards Queens, the borough where Shea Stadium stood.

Everything was working out as planned — until the SIGN showed up! The SIGN … the joy-crushing, life-altering SIGN straight from the pits of … I remember it like it was yesterday. I still sense the disappointment. I recall the hurt. I feel the tears.

Okay, maybe I am a little over the top, but you've been there, haven't you? You have sensed disappointment, known the hurt, felt the tears. Our "flight plan" needs to include instructions for dealing with disappointment. What do we do when we are rejected? What do we do when the sign tells us SOLD OUT? How do we keep our faith when disappointed? More specifically, why should I trust the Lord when I don't get what I want?

I hope you will read this chapter and be encouraged. Look at the words and thoughts of Paul. He certainly heard his fair share of no's, and suffered his quota of disappointments, both personally and in his ministry. Acts chapter 16 contains a good example. In the midst of Paul's second missionary journey ...

> *They passed through the Phrygian and Galatian region, having been forbidden by the Holy Spirit to speak the word in Asia; and after they came to Mysia, they were trying to go into Bithynia, and the Spirit of Jesus did not permit them; and passing by Mysia, they came down to Troas. A vision appeared to Paul in the night: A man of Macedonia was standing and appealing to him, and saying, "Come over to Macedonia and help us." When he had seen the vision, immediately we sought to go into Macedonia, concluding that God had called us to preach the gospel to them (Acts 16:6-10).*

Did you catch those phrases? "Forbidden by the Holy Spirit" and "the Spirit of Jesus would not permit them." Talk about hearing a "NO!" Talk about a SIGN of rejection. And yet, somehow, they managed to trust, to believe in and rely on the integrity, ability and strength of Him. How did they do it? How did they trust? Or, better still, what did Paul and his companions **know** that you must come to know if you are going to trust Him when you do not get what you want in life?

I have a confession to make first. I do not know how God said no to Paul. I don't know if He used circumstances, or visions, or other people

… or some other way. I only know that Paul and his companions' "Gate 4" was Asia, and the Spirit said SOLD OUT. *By the way*, God added, *your game is in Europe*. Well, rather than speculate on the *ways* God spoke, and still speaks, I want to focus on what made them trust enough to accept "no" and change their destination. Here are three statements I have memorized through the years for the "no" times.

He Leads — and I Follow

Jesus is my Lord, my Master, and my Leader. I am His disciple. He leads me. I follow Him. I sometimes forget that simple truth.

There are times when the words of my late father still echo in my mind, "Because I said so!" Though my sisters and I often misunderstood his (and Mom's) directives, and very often disliked them, we followed because he was our father. Sometimes, we obey our Heavenly Father for the same reason — because "He said so." Every day I make choices as to what, or who, I follow. So do you.

If you are reading this book, you made the choice to do so. If you are alive and breathing, you are following something or someone. The question is, "Have you made the conscious decision to follow and obey Jesus as Lord?"

He *Knows* — and I *Think* I Know

The second statement I want to share is "He knows and I think I know." I need to admit that the Lord knows. I only *think* I know. I have been a know-it-all my entire life. Through the years, I have been reminded of this fact. (Usually, I am reminded through the words or looks of my three sisters.) My parents occasionally made mention of this trait, also. Hey, I admit it! I will say, however, I'm not alone! I am a know-it-all who grew up in a home of know-it-alls, who has been blessed with two children who have shown the know-it-all trait. The only one in the household who's not a know-it-all is my wife, Donna. (I may be a know-it-all, but I'm not stupid!) In addition, I can safely say I pastor a congregation of know-it-alls in a city of know-it-alls who dwell in a state of know-it-alls! I suspect it is human nature to believe we can completely map out our lives. Most, if not all, of us are tempted to think we know what is best for our lives. However, as my Grandma Pearl used to say, "Be careful what you wish for." She understood something in her old age: We don't always know what is best.

Remember the story of the Phrygian King Midas? He was granted a wish by Dionysus. Everything he touched turned to gold. His love for gold dimmed his ability to see what was really best. He thought he knew — until his embrace made his loved ones become lifeless and his touch made his food inedible. He discovered what is known today as "the law of unintended consequences," deemed so by sociologist Robert Merton.[15] Sometimes, getting what we want is not the best thing.

The Bible, however, takes a different approach to "know-it-all-ism." Biblical scriptures insist that the Lord knows what's best for His children. "Trust in the Lord with all your heart, and lean not on your own understanding; In all your ways acknowledge Him, and He will direct your paths" (Proverbs 3:5-6, NKJV). Don't get me wrong. I am not against planning. I believe in visioning, dreaming and long-range goal setting. I affirm the old adage, "Those who fail to plan, plan to fail." As a matter of fact, as I write this chapter, I am working on my own Personal 15-Year Life Plan. Yes, I am in favor of planning, with the following caveat: *The Lord knows best, and has both "veto" and "amendment" power over my plans.* He is the One and Only "Know-It-All" — and I trust Him!

Lest you think I am some super Christian, or that I am out of touch with reality, you need to know the *real* me. I am thoroughly human. In fact, I am somewhat self-centered. It has taken me five decades of life, two bouts with cancer and chemotherapy, and several million failures to reach the point of yielding to God's plans, and I still struggle with it.

HE KNOWS — AND I AM SHORTSIGHTED

Finally, I need to remember: He knows, while I am shortsighted. I must rely upon His vision of the future. Perhaps you are familiar with the story and movie *The Hiding Place*. It tells the story of Corrie Ten Boom, who courageously survived the Nazi concentration camps. God has used the experiences from World War II to influence and encourage many hurting people, even to this day.

Let me share with you the words of one of the people touched by Corrie Ten Boom's testimony. Today he is a pastor in Washington, D.C.:

> *Corrie used to speak to audiences of her horrific experiences in the concentration camps, and she would look down while she talked. She wasn't reading her notes. She was actually working on a piece of needlepoint. After sharing about the doubt and anger and pain she experienced, Corrie would reveal the needlepoint. She would hold up the backside of the needlepoint to reveal a jumble of colors and threads with no discernible pattern. And she'd say, 'This is how we see our lives.' Then she would turn the needlepoint over to reveal the design on the other side. Corrie would conclude by saying, 'This is how God views your life, and someday we will have the privilege of viewing it from His point of view.' Corrie could have questioned why she had to suffer. It didn't make sense. It was unfair. But what I do know is this: Somehow God used the suffering of a woman in Holland in 1944 to lead a five-year-old boy named*

Mark Batterson (living in Minneapolis, Minnesota) to Christ more than thirty years later.[16]

Yes, God sees the future, even in the midst of our struggle and disappointment. He has the unique ability to make something good come of both. By the way, as a side note, I had the opportunity to go back to Shea Stadium. Daddy and I went to Helmet Day the next year. When the seventh inning stretch came, I stood with thousands of other kids and waved my helmet for the cameras! Yes, I got the helmet! I got the hot dog! I got the Cracker Jacks! Mostly, I got the joy of spending the day with a father I loved, watching a team I loved playing the game I loved. I sometimes wonder if the apostle Paul questioned God's direction in his life. Did he ever think, as I am prone to think: *Why are You stopping my plans? Why are You not answering the way I'd like? Why can't I have what I want? Why?*

Although I am not sure Paul questioned his Lord, I am certain he obeyed Him. Paul changed his plan (Asia) and headed for Macedonia (Europe). I'm glad he did! Because he went to Europe, the gospel went to Europe. Because the gospel went to Europe, all of history changed. More importantly, my history changed. Over the course of a couple of thousand years, the gospel has made it to our country. As a nineteen-year-old, I heard the good news that love and forgiveness could be mine in Christ. I was saved, my life was changed, and the direction of my future was altered! I am grateful that Paul trusted Him. And I am grateful for the millions of other decisions made throughout the course of church history. From the early church fathers to the Pilgrims and their decisions to trust Him, they all insured my future. Mostly, I am thankful to God. He is the One who is ... who knows ... who sees! And I trust Him! So can you — even if you have to wait a little while for the helmet.

Philippians 3:12-14

Not that I have already obtained it or have already become perfect, but I press on so that I may lay hold of that for which also I was laid hold of by Christ Jesus. Brethren, I do not regard myself as having laid hold of it yet; but one thing I do, forgetting what lies behind and reaching forward to what lies ahead, I press on toward the goal for the prize of the upward call of God in Christ Jesus.

10

ON YOUR MARK! GET SET! GROW!

Although Donna's and my children are now young adults, they remain our children. We have watched the two of them grow from infants to adults. I still remember taking them to the doctor's office for their well-baby checkups. The doctor would examine their hips, arms and legs to make sure they were making the progress they should be making. He would weigh and measure them. He would look into their ears and eyes and check for ... well ... ears and eyes.

As young parents, words like "percentile" and "development" took on new meaning. We became concerned when the percentiles were not what we thought they should be, or when the doctor wanted to talk about "slow development." Growth was a big deal. It still is. In fact, most businesses and organizations are deeply concerned with growth. Growth was, and is, a big deal.

I will state again: We are not born knowing how to fly. We have to *grow* into the role. We have to do the work, check the progress, and adjust the effort in order to reach the goal of flight. I am speaking of *inner* growth, encompassing the intellectual, emotional and spiritual realms. I am afraid we do not take growth seriously enough, or worse yet, we take it for granted. Through my years of dealing with people,

I have discovered some areas of wrong thinking regarding personal development or growth. Perhaps some of you need to un-learn some of this wrong thinking before you can deal with positive growth principles.

One area of flawed thinking is to believe that **some are called to grow while others are not.** Some believe growth is for the super spiritual people. You may say to yourself, *I am a believer in Christ, but my life hasn't changed very much. Growth is just not my thing.* The truth is, we are **all** called to grow spiritually. Our lives with Christ are a journey, taken together. I am amazed by the number of people who have been believers for years, sometimes decades, and still struggle with the same weaknesses. I am not talking about addictions and medical problems, or other major life issues. I'm talking about the struggles that come with character immaturity, which can only be defeated as one grows in Christ. For example, some of us struggle with temper problems and selfish ambition, and seem to have made very little progress. Though we will never achieve perfection in this life, we ought to do better as we grow.

A second error we make regarding spiritual maturity is to believe that **the more gifted you are, the faster you grow**. This is simply not true. Instead, I have my own theory. I believe just the opposite. The less gifted you are, the faster you will grow (provided you take the steps necessary to grow). The more gifted you are, the more tempted you will be toward self-reliance, rather than God-dependence. I have experienced significant growth in times of weakness.

Next, a wrong idea many of us have is **growth is not fun.** I tried to find a better way of putting this, because I don't want to sound judgmental and stereotypical. I am afraid, however, that most people view spiritual growth as a killjoy, reserved for those "ultra-serious" Christians, those who give up more of the fun things in life. Again, I tend to believe the opposite. I have often said to crowds (especially if they're non-church crowds) two things: First, the church includes some of the most ill-tempered, unhappy people you'll ever meet; and second, the ten most loving, caring, joyful people I have ever met are in the church, too. And it's worth the tradeoff for me.

A final mistake is to believe that **growth is automatic, and it takes no investment.** On the surface, it makes sense. We look at our children. They appear to grow naturally, so we assume that age and growth are the same things. But this view of growth is flawed, too. In fact, children do not grow naturally. Age does not mean growth! Occasionally, the local or national news will air a rescue story of a neglected, abused and ignored child. Sadly, these episodes occur more frequently than they used to — tragic stories of children locked in rooms or tied to their beds and shut off from the outside world, with terrible consequences. On most occasions, the "rescued" child is seriously underdeveloped. Has aging taken place? Yes, absolutely. Has growth? Absolutely not. The same is true spiritually. Growth is not automatic. It doesn't just happen. It takes investment. There is nothing worthwhile that doesn't take effort. There is nothing great that doesn't require sacrifice.

Few things of significance can be accomplished without investment. Dr. Ruth is attributed with calling it the "10,000 Hour Theory." To be great at anything, one must devote around 10,000 hours to it. That means, before we ever saw Lebron James dunk a basketball (and before he made his first million dollars), he had worked long and hard. Before my oncologist ever met me or received a dime of salary, he had spent years studying, working and practicing. Greatness comes at a price.

Growth takes investment. What types of investments? What are the elements of spiritual growth? The apostle Paul speaks of his walk (and growth) in terms of the four basic elements of life. A commitment to growth, with the goal of flying, will require investment in each of these areas.

Know Your Past and Deal With It

Spiritual growth is a journey. Like reading a map, one must begin at the starting point. Your growth requires an open and honest look at your starting point — your past. Paul used the phrase "what lies behind" (Philippians 3:13) to describe the perspective needed to accept and deal with one's past. Gordon McDonald, in his book, *A Resilient Life,* calls this "squeezing the past for all its wisdom."[17] Robert Lewis, of Men's Fraternity fame, refers to this as "unpacking." In Tim Coker's everyday vocabulary, I am referring to the ability to take an honest look at mistakes made, wounds received, and blessings given. Mostly, I want to see how my mistakes, my wounds, and my blessings have made me who I am.

What lessons have I learned? How has my past impacted my identity? This involves looking at my family of origin, events (both good and bad) that have shaped my thinking and my personality traits. One of my mentors often states, "Self-awareness is a leader's biggest tool." I must understand my past to become self-aware. This can take time. For some, dealing with the past involves pain. Outside help, from a mentor or counselor, might be necessary. This is heavy stuff, but intentional growth demands this process.

Change Your Perspective and Delete It

Now that you understand your past and have become more self-aware, next you need to learn the art of "forgetting what lies behind" (Philippians 3:13). "Tim, are you crazy? Are we to process or forget?" *Sounds like a contradiction,* you may be thinking. *So which is it?* The simple answer to your question is both. We are to both process and forget our pasts. We should remember and learn from our past, but move beyond it. God wants us to *deal* with our past, but not *dwell* on it.

Few things are sadder than encountering someone who has not been able to move beyond the hurts, hang-ups and disappointments of the past. Please do not misunderstand me. I am not trying to minimize your hurts (I know people who have monumental hurts and disappointments); I am just saying you will not find wholeness until you learn to move on. You can learn to *delete* the past and *move on*. You can learn to fly!

While maturing from childhood to adulthood, we do this all the time, almost naturally. We remember learned lessons and experiences from our past as we live life on a more mature level.

As the only boy in our household, my older sisters picked, harassed or tortured me quite a bit. One of the things they told me was that a family of witches lived on the dark side of the moon. These witches were relatively friendly, unless you angered them, and then they would visit your bedroom at night. As a four- or five-year-old, I really believed them — I mean, really believed them! I couldn't sleep. I was frightened, or as the King James Version of the Bible puts it, I was "sore afraid" (Luke 2:9). Eventually, I dealt with my fear, logically changed my perspective and moved on. My point is, I still *remember* the witches — I just choose to *forget* them!

Allow me another illustration. As a young boy, I was convinced all girls (except my mother and grandmothers) had germs. These germs were called different names, depending on what geographical region I currently lived in. Holding a girl's hand was to invite infection, and to kiss a girl was to welcome death! The longer the kiss, the shorter your life expectancy! I really believed that — until I dealt with my feelings, developed a new perspective, and moved to another maturity level. By the way, I soon learned that kissing girls wasn't all that bad!

These are two silly illustrations, but my point is valid: Though I still remember those old thoughts, experiences and prejudices, I have changed my perspective and deleted them. So can you. It won't always be easy, it may even require some help, but a new level of health and life are waiting on the other side. So, delete it!

Check Your Passion and Drive Toward It

"You're going to need a bigger boat."
"Nobody puts baby in a corner."
"Here's looking at you, kid."

These are among the top 300 most famous movie quotes. But they are *more* than *just* movie quotes; they are summary statements which bring to mind the entirety of the films they represent. When the apostle Paul states, "This one thing I do" (v. 13), he is giving us one of his summary statements. It is a statement of *quality,* not *quantity,* and summarizes the entirety of his life's work. History remembers Paul *doing* many things — author, pastor, mentor and missionary — so, he could not be referring to doing *only* one thing. Paul meant something else: "This one thing I do" refers to intensity, focus, concentration — or PASSION!

A few years ago, Donna and I decided to get serious about our physical condition. We talked with a friend of ours who happened to be a trainer in the local gym. She prescribed a twelve-week workout plan. She met with us for four days and taught us how to safely use the necessary equipment, and then left us on our own. It was incredible! We awoke each day at 5:30 a.m. We recorded our efforts on printouts, which we turned in to her weekly. We changed our diet. We began to read about physical fitness. We began to pray about fitness and a healthy lifestyle. We even began to talk with others about their health. It was the driving passion of our lives for that time. Getting in shape was our "one thing." Now, we didn't stop ministering, teaching, parenting or going about our normal life. We simply shifted our focus.

What is the driving passion of your life? What is your "one thing"? Are you investing your time, energy and resources toward that one thing? If you are to grow, these questions must be asked — and answered.

It's His Purpose, So Dial In To It

Did you hear Paul's words in our passage, "Reaching forward and I press on toward the goal for the prize of the upward call of God"? (Philippians 3:13-14). Those are statements of direction, and speak of purpose. After all the processing and passion are finished, there is the realization that everything we are, and will ever grow to be, falls under the umbrella of God's plan and purpose. As Rick Warren reminds us in *The Purpose Driven Life*, it is not about you.[18] Or, as one kind elderly lady told me years ago (on the occasion of me announcing my intention to enter full-time vocational ministry): Your life is not your own.

If the first three areas of personal growth deal with our past and present, then this last area deals with the future. It calls us to keep going. It urges us to finish strong. By now, you know I am a big sports fan. Few things are worse, as far as sports are concerned, than watching your team not finish well. Whether it is baseball (your team loses the game in the ninth inning), football (you lose the lead after the two-minute warning), golf (he lost the lead on the 72nd hole); sick are the sports fans whose first words in the car leaving the stadium are, "We should have won that game ... but we lost!" Whether we are talking about ministry, family, vocation or vacation, we don't want to hear the words spoken of us, "He/she could have won, but he/she lost." This is about God's purpose and future. Finish strong!

Donna handed me a book one day entitled *Monday Morning Leadership* by David Cotrell. It tells the story of Jeff, a struggling young leader, who seeks out the wisdom of a successful executive named Tony. Over the course of eight Monday morning meetings, the executive guides the young businessman into a path of improvement, both personally and professionally. During their last meeting, Tony challenges Jeff to avoid a life of "Ground Hog Days." The conversation is as follows:

> *Did you see the movie Ground Hog Day — the one where Bill Murray lives the same day over and over again? Yes, pretty funny movie, I said. Well, that's the way many people live their lives, Tony explained. They wake up and do the same things over and over and over — because that's where they are comfortable — until they retire. Jeff, you have too much potential to be living Ground Hog Day over and over ... For you to be the very best, you cannot allow yourself to become complacent in your comfort zone. You need to be reaching for improvement.*[19]

Sounds to me as if Paul could have spoken those words. "Reaching forward to what lies ahead" sounds a lot like "You need to be reaching for improvement." Let me add my words to David Cotrell's and the apostle Paul's: Please do not settle for a path that will not produce growth. Strive for it. Press toward it. Process your past, delete what you need to delete, live with passion and pursue God's purpose for your life!

START TODAY!

How about it? Are you ready to grow? On your Mark ... Get Set ... Grow!

Matthew 14:22-33

Immediately He made the disciples get into the boat and go ahead of Him to the other side, while He sent the crowds away. After He had sent the crowds away, He went up on the mountain by Himself to pray; and when it was evening, He was there alone. But the boat was already a long distance from the land, battered by the waves; for the wind was contrary. And in the fourth watch of the night He came to them, walking on the sea. When the disciples saw Him walking on the sea, they were terrified, and said, "It is a ghost!" And they cried out in fear. But immediately Jesus spoke to them, saying, "Take courage, it is I; do not be afraid." Peter said to Him, "Lord, if it is You, command me to come to You on the water." And He said, "Come!" And Peter got out of the boat, and walked on the water and came toward Jesus. But seeing the wind, he became frightened, and beginning to sink, he cried out, "Lord, save me!" Immediately Jesus stretched out His hand and took hold of him, and said to him, "You of little faith, why did you doubt?" When they got into the boat, the wind stopped. And those who were in the boat worshiped Him, saying, "You are certainly God's Son!"

11

WHAT DO YOU DO WITH GHOSTS?

"The winds come up, and everything changes!" Those were the words spoken by an Israeli pool attendant on our trip to the Holy Land. Having been to the Sea of Galilee, I have experienced the evening storms. The daytime hours of still, unyielding heat give way to evening winds coming over the mountains, and suddenly it seems as if you're in another place. Our tour group experienced this disruptive change one evening. After our evening meal, a few members of our group exited the hotel for the pool area, expecting the heat of the day to have mellowed somewhat. We emerged into a cool, dark and blustery windstorm! Dreams of a lazy, hazy tropical evening of leisure quickly gave way to thoughts of temperature, towels and TERROR. We scrambled for our gear and headed to our rooms. "The winds come up, and everything changes!"

Isn't life like that sometimes? Maybe your life was like that today. A storm came up and everything changed. I hope to encourage you in the midst of your storm. I especially desire to speak to your heart if your trouble is a crisis you do not understand.

I have always been fascinated by the story of Jesus walking on the water in the midst of the storm. Specifically, I've always marveled at the disciples' response to Jesus. I do not think the disciples' biggest battle was the wind. They were fishermen. They were used to the Sea of Galilee. They had experienced the winds before, and they knew how to deal with them. Some storms were worse than others, and this one seems to have been a "doozy" (as my mom used to say), but the formula for fighting them remained unchanged. Mark's account of this storm tells us they were "straining at the oars" (Mark 6:48). That's what they did when the storms came up. That's what we do when our storms come up. We pull out the unchanged formulas and strain against the winds of life. Experts call our formulas "coping mechanisms" rather than oars, but the principle is the same: We do whatever it takes to survive the crisis (storm) and then, we return to normal as quickly as possible.

What I want you to consider in this chapter is: What do you do when the storm is not normal? What do you do when the formulas don't work? Specifically, what do you do with a ghost? You see, I believe the disciples were terrified — not of the storm — but of the ghost! They had dealt with storms before, but a ghost? I can just hear Peter screaming, "Jo … Joh … John! It's a GHOST!!" They did not know what to do next. Do you?

What do you do when a trial or crisis comes into your life and makes no sense? What do you do with the unexplained suffering? How do you deal with the negative test result, the undeserved loss or innocent tragedy? What do you do with ghosts?

I do not claim to have all of the answers. I am not even sure I have many words of wisdom. I do, however, have experience dealing with life's ghosts. I also have a genuine burden for those facing one, for those whom the world makes no sense. If you are dealing with a ghost, I hope to encourage you with a few simple statements drawn from Mark's account of the storm, and from my own ghost.

What Do You Do with Ghosts?

Ghosts Are Real, and They Change Everything

First, I would like to tell you about my ghost. I have always believed that life is uncertain, fragile even, but this uncertainty became real about twelve years ago. It came out of nowhere. Our church softball team had just won our league's championship. I was finishing a relaxing summer vacation, looking forward to the fall, South Carolina football, the approaching holidays, and a busy time in our church family. I was in a good place in my life. Except for a swollen place underneath my right ear, I was in the best physical shape I had been in for several years. But my world was about to be turned upside down. The storm was coming, and along with it, my personal ghost. In the course of treating my swollen parotid gland, I was diagnosed with non-Hodgkin's lymphoma.

My first response was, *I'm not going to live until Christmas, and I love Christmas! I'll never see my daughter graduate from high school or my son from college. I won't be able to travel with Donna anymore. I'm not able to handle this burden. I'm going to die.*

The next several weeks were devoted to second opinions at a major medical center, first and second surgical biopsies, second guesses, fear and questions. *If only I could have prevented this. Is it my love for Diet Coke? How about too much Mexican food? Do I need to exercise more? Tell me what to do to stop this ... this* (I could barely say the C word) *from ruining my life!* Nothing made sense to me. Hadn't I been trying to serve the Lord? Hadn't I been a good person? Hadn't I tried to be a good husband? Father? Pastor? Friend? I had many unanswered questions, but one thing I knew: MY LIFE WOULD NEVER BE THE SAME!

One thing you can be sure of when you encounter a situational ghost: Life will never be the same. You will be haunted by the uncertainty of your circumstances. There will be many unanswered questions. There will be times of anger, frustration and fear. Remember this: The disciples were in the boat that night, in a storm, faced with what they thought was a ghost, because they had done exactly what Jesus had asked them to do!

Ghosts Are Real, and So Is the Enemy

Another thing you can be sure of when you encounter a situational ghost is that you will be approached by the enemy. If you are not comfortable believing in the enemy (I haven't always believed in a personal evil being — devil — but have come to believe in him), then substitute the word negativity or fear for this personal evil. The disciples in the boat that night were terrified and cried out in fear (Matthew 14:26).

Fear and negativity are everywhere in our culture. They sneak around the halls of our minds like the Grinch slithers around Christmas trees. Fear and negativity speak in a variety of ways. I had a family member ask me what sin I had committed for God to have given me this disease. Upon entering a restaurant, I saw a child stare at my bald head and ask, "Momma, what's wrong with that man?" The child's words sparked feelings of insecurity. Mostly, however, the negative voice came from within: *You must not be much of a man. You'll certainly fail as a pastor now. People don't really care about you. You are going to die, and they won't even remember you.* My favorite doubtful thought was: *How can you give your life to a God who allows this to happen to one of His children?* Have you ever heard one of those voices in your head? Or have you said the words? Doubtful thoughts will breed in your mind, literally sucking the life out of you if you don't resist them.

Ghosts Are Real, and People Matter

Looking back on my experience with cancer, I would have surrendered to the ghost of doubt and fear had it not been for the encouragement of the people God placed in my path. Note to self: If you are going to get caught in a storm in the middle of the night, flailing along in a small boat, and approached by a ghost ... make sure you are not alone!

I do not have adequate time or space to elaborate on all of the individuals and groups God used to encourage me, but I would like to mention a few of them. I met an oncologist who not only doctored my disease, but also gave me permission to fight and laugh my way through treatment. The staff and nurses at Carolina Healthcare in Florence, South Carolina, cared for me with dignity and joy, which enabled me to keep *my* dignity and joy; the leadership in our congregation washed the feet of our church family while leading prayer vigils on my behalf; the many men of our church who shaved their heads as my hair fell out reminded me I was not alone. My family always treated me with love, even on my bad days. There were cards by the hundreds, phone calls from encouragers, kind words from strangers ... it seemed as if He knew exactly when to send someone to me. If you have a loved one who is fighting this battle (or any battle), let me encourage you to call, write, give and go. Mostly, if you have the opportunity and ability, bring laughter. People who are afraid of ghosts need it. It makes a difference.

Ghosts Are Real, and God Shows Up

I was reminded during my bout with cancer why I answered the call and signed up for ministry years ago: God is real and changes lives. He has a way of showing up in the midst of our pain and fear. He comes to us on the waves, reminding us He is in charge. Peter started toward Him, took his eyes off of Jesus, and sank. But do you think Peter's life was the same after that night? Jesus changes everything! He certainly changed my life. As I went through Rituxan-CHOP chemotherapy, I began each morning saying what Peter discovered out there on the Sea of Galilee, "Lord, unless You save me, I'll perish. My life is in Your hands." It became my cry. It has become my cry. He enabled me to stay relatively strong in the midst of treatment. He enabled me not to miss a Sunday morning from the pulpit. He enabled my family to weather the storm and to make the most of each day. He enabled me, in one deacon's words (in what became one of the nicest things said to me), to model joy in the midst of trial, and He has given me a new appreciation for those who battle the C word (or any other ghost). My cancer is incurable. Science says it will return. But Jesus reminds me that my life is worth living! Don't be afraid of ghosts. Jesus is out there on your waves, calling. Your life is worth living, too!

Isn't it time for you to fly?

Conclusion

Well, it is finally over, and once again Mrs. McAuliffe, my wonderful fifth grade teacher, was right. On the occasion of presenting me with a writing award, she proudly announced to Public School Twenty-Six, "I just know that one day we will walk into a Broadway play or pick up a book written by young Timothy here!"

I want to thank you for picking up this book. I have been working on it for some fifteen years. Much has changed in the time that I have been plodding along. Besides the obvious — our children have grown, I have twice battled cancer and have aged — other things have changed, too.

For one thing, flying is significantly different than it used to be. This shift actually began after the tragedy of 9/11 but has continued into this post-modern world. When I wrote the introduction to this book, frequenting America's airports was viewed as an adventure. Now, extremely long security checks, cancelled flights and other safety concerns have filled some travelers with a sense of dread.

I am certain of two things, however, that I would like to leave with you. First, let me remind you that perspective will make a big difference in your trip. You choose whether or not you have joy in your journey — whether you *travel* or *fly*. It is your choice alone.

Second, remember that the purpose of any trip is to arrive at your destination. Either you are heading to visit somewhere or you are headed home. Home … that is an interesting word, isn't it? It means a special place for some. For others, it is a special feeling. Most would agree with the old cliché: There's no place like home!

I remember coming home from Brazil after one of our church's mission trips. Our team landed in Columbia, South Carolina, after a two-week escapade filled with tiring days of construction and nights spent preaching. We longed to taste our kind of food, watch our kind of television and sleep in our own beds. Mostly, we longed to see our families. I vividly remember looking for the faces of Christopher and Ashton; moreover, I remember them looking for me! Two weeks earlier, I had left them in the same airport terminal crying as I walked through the departure gate. It had been a long two weeks; though I had made myself at home in Brazil, I was not really home. Things were different on this day, however, as I came through the arrival gate. My children met me with familiar hugs and kisses. Then, as if in a fairy tale, I was embraced by the woman of my dreams. Donna welcomed me back. I forgot all about the long days, the sleepless nights and the strange food. I was home!

Your journey is going to end in a homecoming, also. When your life has ended, and you have flown all you can in this world, you'll *Fly Away* (to use the words of the old gospel song). I am not sure how long before your flight lands, but I can assure you one thing: There's someone waiting. In heaven, we will be reunited with our loved ones. I believe heaven is a real place where we will live for eternity, together. When we arrive, I can see our family and friends gathering to welcome me. There will be hugs and kisses. I will forget about the long days, the sleepless nights, the disease, the suffering and losses I experienced. I'll even forget some of the food! Mostly, I believe the One, and Only One, worth living for will be there. I'll see Him as I walk through the gate. He'll be waiting for me! I'll see His eyes and feel His embrace. I'll be welcomed. I'll really be home!

Notes

1. Spiros Zodhiates, *The Hebrew-Greek Key Study Bible* (AMG Publishers, 1984), 1633

2. King Duncan Jr., *Dynamic Preaching* (Knoxville: Seven Worlds Publisher) Volume XVIV, No. 1, 73

3. Paul Lee Tan, *Encyclopedia of 7,700 Illustrations* (Rockville: Assurance Publishing, 1979), 439

4. Walter B. Knight, editor, *Knights Master Book of Illustrations* (Grand Rapids: Eerdmans Publishing House, 1987), 86

5. "Fatal Overreaction" *Time*, 14 August 1989, 33 cited in Craig Brian Larson, *Engaging Illustrations for Preachers, Teachers and Writers* (Grand Rapids: Baker Books, 1993), 169

6. Charles Swindoll, *The Inspirational Writings of Charles Swindoll, Living Above the Level of Mediocrity* (New York: Inspirational Press, 1987), 42

7. Wayne Rice, editor, *Hot Illustrations for Youth Talks* (El Cajon: Youth Specialties, Inc., 1994), 230

8. Rick Warren, "Purpose Driven Preaching" (presented at the Purpose Driven Pastors Gathering, Saddleback Community Church, March 2, 1999).

9. Wayne Rice, *Hot Illustrations for Youth Talks*, 230

10. Charles Dickens, *Great Expectations* (1859)

11. Quoted by Charles Swindoll, *The Tale of the Tardy Oxcart* (Nashville: Word Publishing, Inc., 1998), 216

12. Source unknown, attributed to Harvard psychologist Jerome Bruner in *The Quotable Coach*

13. Jim Henry, *The Pastor's Wedding Manual* (Nashville: Broadman Press, 1985), 162

14. William Barclay, *Barclay's Daily Study Bible, Revised Edition, Galatians and Ephesians* (Philadelphia: Westminster Press, 1976), 178

15. Mark Batterson, *In a Pit with a Lion on a Snowy Day* (Colorado Springs: Multnomah Books, 2005), 65

16. Ibid. 98

17. Gordon MacDonald, *A Resilient Life* (Nashville: Thomas Nelson, 2006), 136

18. Rick Warren, *The Purpose Driven Life* (Grand Rapids: Zondervan, 2002), 17

19. David Cottrell, *Monday Morning Leadership* (Dallas: Cornerstone Leadership Institute, 2016), 13

www.ingramcontent.com/pod-product-compliance
Lightning Source LLC
LaVergne TN
LVHW051844080426
835512LV00018B/3066